Vocabulary
in Context

FOR THE COMMON CORE STANDARDS

Grade
9

Table of Contents

Introduction 4
Determining Meaning Through Word Analysis
  Prefixes 5
  Suffixes 6
  Roots and Word Families 7

Unit 1
Wood Rat Laughs at Rattlesnake Venom .. 8
Context Clues 10
Word Maze 12
Standardized Test Practice 13
Understanding Multiple-Meaning Words 14
Understanding Related Words 15
The Latin Root *pon/pos* 16
Completing Sentences 16
Writing 17

Unit 2
Flying with the Sun 18
Context Clues 19
Understanding Multiple-Meaning Words 20
Cloze Paragraphs 20
Synonyms and Antonyms 21
The Greek Root *mono* 21
Word Game 22
Challenge Yourself 22
Standardized Test Practice 23
Understanding Related Words 24
Antonyms 25
Writing Sentences 25
Completing Sentences 26
Writing 27

Unit 3
A Bridge to America 28
Context Clues 29
Analogies 30
Word Pairs 30
Word Game 31
Crossword Puzzle 32

Standardized Test Practice 33
Understanding Related Words 34
Synonyms and Antonyms 35
Dictionary Skills 35
Completing Sentences 36
Writing 37

Unit 4
The Cajuns 38
Context Clues 40
Matching Ideas 42
True-False 42
Standardized Test Practice 43
Understanding Related Words 44
Dictionary Skills 44
The Latin Root *vert* 45
Challenge Yourself 45
Word Pairs 46
Forming Words 46
Writing 47

Unit 5
Statues That Wait 48
Context Clues 49
Understanding Multiple-Meaning Words 50
Word Groups 50
Word Map 51
Synonyms and Antonyms 52
The Suffixes *–able* and *–ible* 52
Standardized Test Practice 53
Understanding Related Words 54
Word Groups 55
Word Pairs 55
Synonyms 56
Writing 57

Unit 6
All Gold Canyon 58
Context Clues 60
Using Context Clues 62

Figures of Speech 62
Standardized Test Practice 63
Understanding Related Words 64
Answering Questions About Words 65
The Prefix *in-* 65
Understanding Multiple-Meaning Words 66
Writing 67

Unit 7

Cave Hunters, Beware! 68
Context Clues...69
Dictionary Skills 70
Rewriting Sentences.................................70
Word Map..71
Yes or No? 72
Challenge Yourself...................................72
Standardized Test Practice 73
Understanding Related Words 74
Analogies 75
Word Pairs 75
Word Game...76
Writing 77

Unit 8

Bill Cosby Gives It Up 78
Context Clues..79
Word Game..80
Understanding Multiple-Meaning Words 81
True-False...82
Challenge Yourself...................................82
Standardized Test Practice 83
Understanding Related Words 84
Antonyms 85
Name Game 85
Word Origins 86
Writing Sentences 86
Writing 87

Unit 9

Fighting Germs 88
Context Clues...89
Rewriting Sentences.................................90
True-False...90
Understanding Multiple-Meaning Words 91
Word Groups...92
Challenge Yourself 92
Standardized Test Practice 93
Understanding Related Words 94
Antonyms 95
Dictionary Skills 95
Completing Sentences 96
Writing 97

Unit 10

The Railroad Excursion............................98
Context Clues..99
Word Game 100
Understanding Multiple-Meaning Words ...101
Standardized Test Practice 103
Understanding Related Words 104
Analogies..105
Word Descriptions 105
Cloze Sentences.....................................106
Writing 107

Glossary 108

Answer Key 117

Introduction

Steck-Vaughn's *Vocabulary in Context* series offers parents and educators high-quality, curriculum-based products that align with the Common Core Standards for English Language Arts for grades 2–9.

Each unit in the *Vocabulary in Context* books includes:

- fiction and/or nonfiction selections, covering a wide variety of topics

- context activities, ascertaining that students understand what they have read

- vocabulary activities, challenging students to show their understanding of key vocabulary

- questions in a standardized-test format, helping prepare students for standardized exams

- word skills activities, targeting additional vocabulary words and vocabulary skills

- writing activities, providing assignments that encourage students to use the vocabulary words

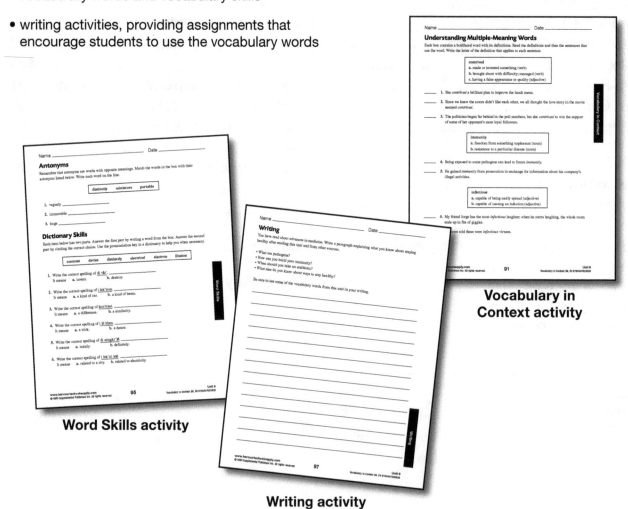

Reading selection

Vocabulary in Context activity

Word Skills activity

Writing activity

Vocabulary in Context G9, SV 9780547625829

Determining Meaning Through Word Analysis

Words are made up of various combinations of the following parts: prefix, suffix, base word, and root. Analysis of these parts is another way to determine an unfamiliar word's meaning.

Prefix   a word part that is added to the beginning of another word or word part
Suffix   a word part that is added to the end of another word or word part
Base Word   a complete word to which a prefix and/or a suffix may be added
Root   a word part to which a prefix and/or a suffix must be added. A root cannot stand alone.

Prefixes

Prefix	Meaning	Example
a-, ab-	up, out; not; away	arise; abnormal; absent
anti-	against; prevents, cures	antiaircraft; antidote
contra-	opposed	contradict
de-	away from, off; down; reverse action of	derail; decline; defrost
dis-	lack of; not; away	distrust; dishonest; disarm
equi-	equal	equidistant
il-, im-, in-, ir-	not; in, into	illegal; investigate
inter-	between, among	international
mal-	bad	maltreat, malignant
mis-	wrong	misspell
non-	not	nonworking
post-	after in time or space	postpone
pre-	before	predawn
pro-	in favor of; forward, ahead	profamily; propel
re-	again; back	rethink; repay
semi-	half; twice in a period; partly	semicircle; semiannual; semiconscious
sub-	under, below	subzero
trans-	across; beyond	transcontinental; transcend
un-	not; reverse of	unhappy; unfasten

Suffixes

Noun Suffixes

Suffix	Example	Suffix	Example
-ance, -ancy, -ence	vigilance, vacancy, independence	-ism	realism, federalism
-ant	commandant, occupant	-ist	geologist
-ation, -ion, -ition	imagination, inspection, recognition	-ity, -ty	sincerity, frailty
-cy	accuracy	-ment	encouragement, commitment
-eer, -er	auctioneer, manager	-ness	kindness, fondness
-hood	womanhood, brotherhood	-or	counselor
-ice	cowardice, prejudice	-ship	ownership, worship
-ician	beautician, statistician	-tude	gratitude, solitude

Adjective Suffixes

Suffix	Meaning	Example
-able, -ible	able to be	readable, convertible
-al, -ant, -ar	relating to	musical, triumphant, polar
-ate	having, full of	passionate
-ful	full of	harmful
-ic, -ish	pertaining to, like	heroic, foolish
-ive	pertaining to	descriptive
-less	without	senseless
-like, -ly	like	lifelike, scholarly
-most	at the extreme	topmost
-ous	full of	furious
-or	one who	actor
-y	state of	funny

Verb Suffixes

Suffix	Meaning	Example
-ate, -fy	to make	activate, simplify
-en, -ise, -ize	to become	strengthen, merchandise, computerize

Adverb Suffixes

Suffix	Meaning	Example
-ily, -ly	manner	happily, quickly
-ward	toward	skyward
-wise	like	clockwise

Roots and Word Families

A word root cannot stand alone but must be combined with other word parts. A great many roots used in our language come from Greek or Latin. A single root can generate many English words.

Useful Greek Roots

Root	Meaning	Example
aster, astr	star	asterisk
auto	self, alone	autobiography
bibl, biblio	book	bibliography
bi, bio	life	biology
chron	time	chronology
cracy, crat	rule, government	democracy
gram, graph	write, draw, describe	grammar, paragraph
meter, metr	measure	barometer
neo	new	neoclassical
ortho	straight, correct	orthodontist, orthodox
phob	fear	claustrophobia
phon	sound	phonograph
psych	mind, soul, spirit	psychology
scope	see	telescope
tele	far, distant	television
therm	heat	thermometer

Useful Latin Roots

Root	Meaning	Example
capt, cept	take, have	capture, accept
cede, ceed, cess	go, yield, give way	secede, proceed, recess
dic, dict	speak, say, tell	dictate, dictionary
duc, duct	lead	introduce, conductor
fact, fect	do, make	factory, defect
ject	throw, hurl	eject, inject
mob, mot, mov	move	mobility, motion, movie
pon, pos, posit	place, put	opponent, deposit
port	carry	porter, portable
puls	throb, urge	pulsate, compulsory
scrib, script	write	prescribe, scripture
tain, ten, tent	hold	contain, tenant, attention
ven, vent	come	convention, event
vers, vert	turn	versatile, invert
vid, vis	see	video, vista
voc, vok	voice, call	vocal, invoke

Wood Rat Laughs at Rattlesnake Venom

by James Coomber

Read the selection. Think about the meanings of the **boldfaced** words. Then go back to the selection. Underline the words or sentences that give you a clue to the meaning of each **boldfaced** word.

John Perez, a biological researcher, uncovered an unexpected relationship in nature. In the case of the rattlesnake and the wood rat, Perez found that "good immunity makes good neighbors."

Even in a housing shortage, few people would want to room with a poisonous rattlesnake. Nevertheless, a common southwestern **rodent**, the wood rat, finds the Western diamondback rattler an acceptable **burrow** mate. Researchers at Texas A&M University—Kingsville have discovered that it is the wood rat's blood chemistry, not **temperament**, that allows this **particular** cohabitation.

Observations that wood rats can survive **multiple** rattlesnake bites **prompted** the laboratory experiments. First, the researchers obtained **venom** from caged rattlesnakes. Then, John Perez and his **colleagues** injected rodents with various **dilutions** of rattlesnake venom, as well as the full-strength venom. They found that two milliliters of full-strength venom is required to kill half of a sample group of wood rats. This dose is 140 times larger than that needed to kill the same **proportion** of mice.

"The natural **resistance** in wood rats is not surprising," says Perez, "since wood rats and rattlesnakes live in the same **habitat**—often in the same burrows."

Does that mean no wood rat ever dies from a rattler bite? Not exactly. "There is no good way to measure the amount of venom released in a rattlesnake bite," Perez says. "A large rattlesnake could release three milliliters. So a large snake could kill a wood rat, but a small snake couldn't."

Vocabulary in Context G9, SV 9780547625829

The researchers then went on to see if they could transfer the wood rat's **immunity** to venom to another animal. Perez and coworkers removed the cells from wood rat blood and injected half a milliliter of the resulting serum[1] into mice. The experiment was a success. "The mice could then withstand about three times the amount of venom," Perez says.

The scientists are now working to discover what **factor** in the wood rat's blood protects against the venom. **Preliminary** experiments indicate that the substance, whatever it is, does not fight the poison head-on, like a vaccine. Mixing wood rat serum and venom does not produce the same kind of chemical activity that mixing venom and vaccine does. The anti-**lethal** factor in the blood may instead be an enzyme[2] that breaks down the venom **components**.

Perez is not looking only at the wood rat these days. Snakes are typically resistant to their own venom, and Perez also finds immunity in the Mexican ground squirrel, a fierce rodent that can kill a rattlesnake. He **proposes** that factors isolated in these and other studies will be useful in snakebite treatment. "Venom is a very complex **toxin**. It destroys muscle and affects blood," Perez explains. That makes it dangerous and difficult to combat. However, the answer may just lie in nature's own laboratory. The most **effective** weapons against snakebites may be substances taken from the blood of rodents and from the rattlesnakes themselves.

[1] serum: a blood fluid used as an antitoxin, taken from an animal made immune to a specific disease by inoculation

[2] enzyme: a protein-like substance formed in plant and animal cells that helps in starting or speeding up chemical changes in other substances

   Vocabulary in Context G9, SV 9780547625829

Name _____ Date _____

Context Clues

For each sentence write the letter of the word or phrase that is closest in meaning to the word or words in italics. Use context clues to help you choose the correct answer.

_____ 1. A squirrel lives in a hollow tree and a bear lives in a cave, while a rabbit digs a *burrow* in the ground.

    A dirt   **B** hole   **C** wall   **D** carrot

_____ 2. Mr. Del Rio got along very well with the other employees at the library; they were his *colleagues*, and they were also his friends.

    A enemies   **B** neighbors   **C** fellow workers   **D** close relatives

_____ 3. The online store sells all the *components* of the computer, including software and an external hard drive.

    A brands   **B** tools   **C** parts   **D** instructions

_____ 4. The lemonade was so strong that Andrea added more water to it, making a *dilution* of the drink.

    A mess   **B** weaker version   **C** thicker version   **D** medicine

_____ 5. Hammers are not designed for cracking nuts, but they can be *effective*.

    A wrong   **B** typical   **C** useful   **D** useless

_____ 6. The traffic accident was the result of several *factors*, one of which was the wet pavement.

    A causes   **B** systems   **C** methods   **D** surprises

_____ 7. Forests and wooded areas have always been the deer's *habitat*, but deer can also be found in the suburbs.

    A diet   **B** fear   **C** natural family   **D** natural environment

_____ 8. Some people have severe reactions to poison ivy, but others seem to have developed a natural *immunity to* it.

    A attraction to   **B** enjoyment of   **C** protection against   **D** hatred of

_____ 9. Carbon monoxide can be *lethal*, causing death in a very short period of time.

    A deadly   **B** unpleasant   **C** healthful   **D** useful

_____ 10. A rosebush does not produce only one flower; it has *multiple* blossoms.

    A many   **B** complicated   **C** beautiful   **D** scented

        Vocabulary in Context G9, SV 9780547625829

_____ **11.** There were hundreds of books of all kinds on the shelves, but the *particular* one she wanted was not there.

    A typical   **B** specific   **C** fictional   **D** duplicate

_____ **12.** In *preliminary* rehearsals for a play, actors may not yet know all their lines, and the stage may be just a room with a few folding chairs.

    A quick   **B** beginning   **C** efficient   **D** final

_____ **13.** Peggy's need for extra money *prompted* her search for a job.

    A prevented   **B** caused   **C** delayed   **D** ended

_____ **14.** When he asked what *proportion* of our team had scored in the last game, I said I thought it was about half.

    A leader   **B** strategy   **C** member   **D** fraction

_____ **15.** Ms. Hernández asked for possible solutions to the litter problem. Joel *proposed* that more trash cans be put on the school grounds.

    A suggested   **B** demanded   **C** proved   **D** complained

_____ **16.** Because Vern's *resistance* was low, he quickly caught the flu from his brother.

    A eligibility   **C** ability to get medication

    B ability to fight illness   **D** integrity

_____ **17.** Rats, mice, squirrels, and other *rodents* all have large front teeth with which they do much chewing.

    A gnawing mammals   **C** dangerous mammals

    B pets   **D** animals

_____ **18.** In trying to understand why Tom got so angry, you must consider his *temperament*; he's just an angry sort of person.

    A self-control   **B** nature   **C** patience   **D** illness

_____ **19.** These two mushrooms look very much alike, but the one on the left is harmless, while the one on the right contains a strong *toxin*.

    A flavor   **B** aroma   **C** poison   **D** texture

_____ **20.** The *venom* that some spiders inject into a body quickly flows into the bloodstream, causing pain, swelling, and sometimes death.

    A stinger   **B** powerful medicine   **C** poisonous liquid   **D** soreness

Vocabulary in Context

Word Maze

All the words in the box are hidden in the maze. The words are arranged forward, backward, up, down, and diagonally. Circle each word as you find it and cross the word off the list. Different words may overlap and use the same letter.

burrow	colleagues	components	dilutions	effective
factor	habitat	immunity	lethal	multiple
particular	preliminary	prompt	proportion	propose
resistance	rodent	temperament	toxin	venom

```
A  C  O  L  L  E  A  G  U  E  S  M  F  B
E  R  O  D  E  N  T  P  M  O  R  P  A  O
I  E  M  H  P  A  R  T  I  C  U  L  A  R
X  S  Y  R  A  N  I  M  I  L  E  R  P  B
C  I  E  T  N  B  R  W  P  V  E  N  O  M
O  S  F  O  W  N  I  M  M  U  N  I  T  Y
M  T  F  X  O  L  E  T  H  A  L  U  G  N
P  A  E  I  R  X  A  F  A  C  T  O  R  Z
O  N  C  N  R  Z  M  U  L  T  I  P  L  E
N  C  T  L  U  S  Y  T  A  T  I  B  A  H
E  E  I  H  B  D  I  L  U  T  I  O  N  S
N  N  V  P  R  O  P  O  R  T  I  O  N  C
T  E  E  T  N  E  M  A  R  E  P  M  E  T
S  P  R  O  P  O  S  E  O  X  A  R  L  N
```

Standardized Test Practice

Determine the relationship between the pair of capitalized words. Then decide which other word pair expresses a similar relationship. Circle the letter of the correct pair.

> **TIP**
>
> Always read all the answer choices. Many choices may seem correct. Only one answer choice expresses the same relationship.

1. RAT : RODENT : :

    A canine : dog

    B feline : cat

    C snake : reptile

    D turtle : tortoise

2. PRELIMINARY : EARLY : :

    A lifelike : unrealistic

    B central : outer

    C final : concluding

    D friendly : mean

3. PARTICULAR : GENERAL : :

    A hot : cold

    B difficult : hard

    C exterior : outside

    D childish : childlike

4. BURROW : MOUSE : :

    A cave : bear

    B house : home

    C black : white

    D natural : horse

Circle the letter of the word that is a synonym of the capitalized word.

5. COLLEAGUE

    A brother   **B** friend   **C** athlete   **D** coworker

6. COMPONENT

    A part   **B** company   **C** loss   **D** rival

7. FACTOR

    A machine   **B** element   **C** use   **D** shock

Circle the letter of the word or words that best complete the sentence.

8. If you were to make a *dilution* of a drink, you would

    A water it down.   **B** make it colder.   **C** thicken it.   **D** make it warmer.

9. The word *temperament* refers to a person's

    A career.   **B** clothes.   **C** disposition.   **D** fever.

10. The word *multiple* means

    A many.   **B** one.   **C** none.   **D** two.

Vocabulary in Context

Understanding Multiple-Meaning Words

Each box in this exercise contains a boldfaced word with its definitions. Read the definition and then the sentences that use the word. Write the letter of the definition that applies to each sentence.

> **effective**
> **a.** producing the desired result; useful (adjective)
> **b.** impressive, striking (adjective)
> **c.** in effect, operative, activated (adjective)

_____   **1.** The new dress code is *effective* as of the beginning of the school year.

_____   **2.** Penicillin is highly *effective* in combating a number of serious illnesses.

_____   **3.** That streak of red across the bright white canvas is very *effective*, don't you think?

> **particular**
> **a.** relating to a single person or thing, specific (adjective)
> **b.** concerned with details, picky (adjective)
> **c.** an item of information, a detail of news (noun)

_____   **4.** Oh, I'll wear anything that's in my closet. I'm not *particular*.

_____   **5.** We know all about the game. Andrés gave us the *particulars* when he got home.

_____   **6.** That *particular* plant seems much healthier than the others.

> **prompt**
> **a.** to move to action (verb)
> **b.** to remind someone of forgotten words (verb)
> **c.** quick, instant, unhesitating, without delay (adjective)
> **d.** on time, punctual, not tardy (adjective)

_____   **7.** We're leaving for the party at 7:45. Be *prompt* or be left behind!

_____   **8.** What in the world *prompted* you to dye your hair pink the week before the family reunion?

_____   **9.** Aisha, would you watch the script and *prompt* the actors until they learn their lines?

_____   **10.** A good office worker is always *prompt* in responding to letters and memos.

14

Word Skills

Understanding Related Words

The words in the box are closely related to the vocabulary words. See how many of the words you already know. Use the glossary to find definitions of unfamiliar words.

dilute	effectively	immune	inhabit	inhabitant
nontoxic	promptness	proportional	proposal	toxic

Write the word from the box that best completes the meaning of the sentence.

1. It is sometimes necessary to _____ paint so that it will be thin enough to flow smoothly from the brush.

2. The Roosevelt elk is a(n) _____ of Washington State's rain forests, as are deer, squirrels, and a great many woodpeckers.

3. In Scandinavia, being late is considered extremely rude; _____ is expected of any polite person.

4. A good diet can strengthen the _____ system of the body, making the body more effective in fighting off disease.

5. Garbage that is _____ is dangerous and must be taken to special dumps.

6. Due to the extreme cold, few people _____ the areas around the North and South Poles.

7. A lot of us had suggestions about how to improve the school elections, but Felipe was the only one who presented his _____ to the student council.

8. The committee members worked together _____; in a very short period of time, they came up with several great ideas.

9. In the United States Senate, each state has two senators, but representation in the House is _____, based on the relative populations of the states.

10. All art supplies used by young children should be _____ because children so often put things in their mouths.

Unit 1
Vocabulary in Context G9, SV 9780547625829

Word Skills

The Latin Root *pon/pos*

The words *component* and *propose* come from the Latin *ponere*, meaning "to put" or "to place." *Component* literally means "something placed together" (with other things), and *propose* means "to put forth." The following related words also come from this Latin word (notice the root can be either *pon* or *pos*).

dispose	impose	impostor	opponent	proponent

Match each word on the left with its definition on the right. Write the appropriate letter on the line.

_____ **1.** dispose

_____ **2.** proponent

_____ **3.** impostor

_____ **4.** opponent

_____ **5.** impose

A. someone pretending to be somebody else to cheat or fool

B. to get rid (of)

C. to force

D. someone who argues for or wants something

E. someone who is against a particular action or belief

Completing Sentences

Write the word from the box that best completes the meaning of the sentence.

dispose	impose	impostor	opponent	proponent

1. In a democracy, one party should not be able to use the law to _____ its beliefs on another.

2. Some people thought that the woman named Anastasia was a member of the Russian royal family, but others thought she was a(n) _____.

3. Senator Rosales was willing to debate, but her _____ in the campaign refused.

4. Laws require that hospitals _____ of toxic material very carefully.

5. The main _____ of the bill gave a powerful speech in favor of it.

Word Skills

Writing

Write a short description of the habitat of an animal of your choice.

• In which part(s) of the world does the animal live?
• What is the climate?
• Does the animal change its habitat with the seasons, or does it stay in the same place all year?
• How does the animal's particular habitat aid in the animal's survival?

Be sure to use some of the vocabulary words from this unit in your writing.

_____

_____

_____

_____

_____

_____

_____

_____

_____

_____

_____

Writing

Vocabulary in Context G9, SV 9780547625829

Flying with the Sun

Read the selection. Think about the meanings of the **boldfaced** words. Then go back to the selection. Underline the words or sentences that give you a clue to the meaning of each **boldfaced** word.

Inventor Paul MacCready was a man with a mission—to get people to solve their present-day problems by looking back to the past or forward to the future. One of MacCready's more famous projects did both. His plane, the *Solar Challenger*, looked like something the Wright brothers might have built, but it was designed to operate on the energy of the sun. It was not the first plane to attempt to **harness** solar energy and put it to work, but it was the first to do so without storing the energy in batteries before taking off.

At only 217 pounds, the *Solar Challenger* definitely qualified as **lightweight**. It was a **monoplane**—an aircraft with a single set of wings. It got its power from more than 16,000 solar cells spread over the wings and the rear section of the plane. These cells collected energy from the sun and converted it to electricity, which was then **conducted** through wires to the engine.

The maiden flight of the *Solar Challenger* in 1981 had its ups and downs. On an airport runway in Paris, France, the pilot repeatedly attempted to get the plane off the ground without success. Finally, the aircraft slowly rose into the air. When he saw the **altimeter** reading of 240, the pilot was very relieved. The *Solar Challenger* eventually reached an altitude of 11,000 feet. As the pilot **accelerated** to a speed of forty-seven miles per hour, the plane headed across the English Channel. Powered only by the sun and its own **kinetic** energy—the energy an object has because it is already in motion—the *Solar Challenger* completed its voyage. It landed in Dover, England, five hours and twenty-three minutes after takeoff.

Admittedly, a plane that can fly only when the sun is shining is not very practical. However, the flight of the *Solar Challenger* demonstrated that solar energy is an **accessible** energy source that can be obtained easily. MacCready believed that inventions like his could be **modified**, or changed, for more practical uses. He continued to explore ways to use the sun's power to drive **mechanized**, or machine-run, vehicles, inventing *Sunraycer*, a solar car, and *Gossamer Penguin*, another solar-powered plane. MacCready continued to develop new environmentally sound methods of transporting people until his death in 2007.

Context Clues

Read each sentence. Look for context clues to help you complete each sentence with a word from the box. Write the word on the line.

accessible	accelerated	altimeter	conducted	harness
kinetic	lightweight	mechanized	modified	monoplane

1. In today's _____ society, most work is done by machines.

2. But as more power is needed, people have _____, or altered, their ideas about possible energy sources.

3. Paul MacCready had an idea for an airplane that used the sun's energy and its own _____ energy, the energy of motion, for its power.

4. MacCready had been working slowly on the plane for several years, but when the energy shortage began in the 1970s, he _____ his efforts.

5. Called the *Solar Challenger*, this _____ had only one set of wings.

6. Unlike planes built of heavy materials, the *Solar Challenger* was made of a _____ plastic and weighed only 217 pounds.

7. Special energy cells collected the solar energy and converted it to electricity, which was _____ to the engine.

8. The test pilot flew the plane at a height of 11,000 feet, as measured by the _____, the altitude gauge in the plane.

9. The successful flight of the *Solar Challenger* proved that people can _____, or control and use, the sun's energy.

10. But solar energy is _____ only when the sun shines!

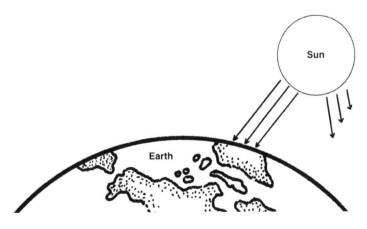

Vocabulary in Context

Understanding Multiple-Meaning Words

The words in the box have more than one meaning. Look for the clues in each sentence to tell which meaning is being used. Write the letter of the correct meaning next to the sentence.

lightweight	harness
a. not heavy (adjective)	**e.** straps used to control an animal (noun)
b. not important (adjective)	**f.** to control and put to work (verb)
conducted	**modified**
c. transmitted (verb)	**g.** changed slightly
d. led a musical group (verb)	**h.** made less extreme or severe

_____ **1.** A windmill can be used to harness the wind.

_____ **2.** In view of all their troubles, my problems are lightweight.

_____ **3.** The copper frying pan conducted the heat evenly.

_____ **4.** We modified our decision and said Lil would be confined to the house for only a week instead of a whole month.

_____ **5.** A famous musician conducted the orchestra.

_____ **6.** Although this is a lightweight aluminum, it is very strong.

_____ **7.** We modified our plans so we would be home a day earlier.

_____ **8.** The mule was fastened to the plow with a harness.

Cloze Paragraphs

Use the words in the box to complete the passage. Then reread the passage to be sure it makes sense.

accelerated	accessible	altimeter	kinetic	monoplane

Marisa's husband gave her a glider trip for Christmas. Marisa never thought that such an experience would be (1) _____ to her. She was elated when they approached the airport and she caught her first glimpse of the (2) _____ tied down in the hangar.

Her moment had finally arrived, and she could feel the breeze race over her face as they (3) _____ after takeoff. After they evened off, the navigator checked the (4) _____ and appeared content with their altitude. Powered only by the wind and its own (5) _____ energy, their glider soared with the eagles for over an hour.

Synonyms and Antonyms

Synonyms are words that have similar meanings, while antonyms are words that have opposite meanings. Look at the words below. If they are synonyms, put a (✓) in the Synonyms column. If they are antonyms, put a (✓) in the Antonyms column.

	Antonyms	Synonyms
1. harness—control	_____	_____
2. accessible—unreachable	_____	_____
3. accelerated—slowed	_____	_____
4. modified—changed	_____	_____
5. lightweight—heavy	_____	_____

The Greek Root *mono*

The Greek root *mono* comes from the Greek word *monos*, which means "single" or "alone." The word *monoplane* contains this root. The words below also contain this root.

monarchy	**monotone**	**monochromatic**	**monocle**	**monogrammed**

1. In old photographs, my great-great uncle wore a _____ over his left eye.

2. England has a limited _____; we hope to catch a glimpse of the royals when we visit London.

3. Sometimes the newscaster speaks in a _____; her voice lulls me to sleep.

4. Their living room was _____; the walls, sofas, and tables were all white.

5. The towels were _____ with the new couple's initials.

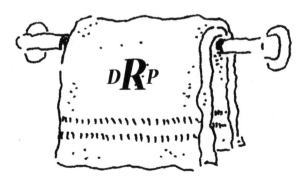

Vocabulary in Context G9, SV 9780547625829

Word Game

Read each clue. Then write the word from the box that fits the clue.

accessible	accelerated	harness	lightweight	modified

1. A windmill must do this to the wind to create energy. _____

2. A person who drove a car faster and faster did this. _____

3. If something has been changed, you could say it has been this. _____

4. A feather could be described as this. _____

5. If you need information that is easy to find, you need this kind of data. _____

Challenge Yourself

1. Name two natural sources of energy that people have been able to harness.

_____

2. Name two things that you have modified.

_____

3. Name something that is mechanized.

_____

Standardized Test Practice

Circle the letter of the word or words that best complete the sentence.

1. An *altimeter* measures an object's

    A altitude.   **B** length.   **C** width.   **D** weight.

2. Something that is *accessible* is

    A worthless.   **B** obtainable.   **C** expensive.   **D** breakable.

3. A *monoplane* has

    A one wheel.   **B** one motion.   **C** one set of wings.   **D** one window.

4. *Kinetic* refers to

    A business.   **B** kindness.   **C** movement.   **D** speech.

5. By building a dam, you can *harness* water's

    A taste.   **B** power.   **C** freshness.   **D** beauty.

6. *Mechanized* work is done by

    A males.   **B** females.   **C** hand.   **D** machines.

7. If a car *accelerated*, it

    A sped up.   **B** slowed down.   **C** turned.   **D** suddenly stopped.

8. *Conducted* electricity is

    A shocking.   **B** ancient.   **C** full.   **D** transmitted.

9. A *modified* plan is

    A approved.   **B** rejected.   **C** shipped.   **D** changed.

10. A *lightweight* material used to make warm-weather clothing is

    A wool.   **B** fur.   **C** cotton.   **D** velvet.

Vocabulary in Context

Understanding Related Words

The words in the box can be related to new technology. They are used here in sentences about satellites. See how many of the words you already know. Use the glossary to find definitions of unfamiliar words.

amazingly	clarity	closeness	contraptions	correspondence
exceeded	humankind	impossibility	overseas	transmit

Use context clues to replace the underlined definition with a word from the box. Write the word on the line. Use the glossary if necessary.

1. Satellites have improved life for much of the people living on Earth.

   _____

2. Satellites send out signals that are picked up by television sets.

   _____

3. These astonishing devices are called Direct Broadcasting Satellites.

   _____

4. Surprisingly, people can set up satellite dishes that are small enough to fit on the roof of a house.

   _____

5. Years ago, watching a live sporting event happening halfway around the world was an event that could not happen.

   _____

6. Now, from the clearness of the image, we cannot tell the broadcast is coming from another continent.

   _____

7. Communications satellites have increased our nearness to the rest of the world.

   _____

8. Before the twentieth century, there was no such thing as an across the ocean telephone call.

   _____

9. Instead, people sent letters and other written messages across the oceans by ship.

   _____

10. Communications satellites allow us to make international phone calls; these satellites have gone beyond the dreams of the pioneers who launched them.

    _____

Word Skills

Antonyms

In each sentence, one word is underlined. That word sounds odd in the sentence. Choose a word from the box that is the antonym of the odd word in the sentence. Write that word on the line.

amazingly	clarity	closeness	impossibility	overseas	transmit

1. _____ : Through sharing their thoughts and feelings, the friends developed a real distance.

2. _____ : You need to fly on a plane to visit your local relatives.

3. _____ : After hundreds of failed attempts at traveling through time, he has finally admitted the possibility of time travel.

4. _____ : The magician unsurprisingly vanished into thin air.

5. _____ : The confusion of her report was impressive.

6. _____ : A television studio can receive a broadcast anywhere in the area.

Writing Sentences

Write an original sentence with each of the words in the box.

contraptions	correspondence	exceeded	humankind

1. _____

_____

2. _____

_____

3. _____

_____

4. _____

_____

Word Skills

Completing Sentences

Write the letter of the word that best completes the sentence.

_____ **1.** *Contraptions* are
   A jokes. **B** toys. **C** devices. **D** plans.

_____ **2.** When you go *overseas*, you travel
   A abroad. **B** near. **C** underwater. **D** quickly.

_____ **3.** The word *amazingly* means
   A remarkably. **B** sadly. **C** confusingly. **D** carefully.

_____ **4.** An author with *clarity* writes
   A quickly. **B** slowly. **C** humorously. **D** clearly.

_____ **5.** People carry on *correspondence* by writing
   A songs. **B** letters. **C** stamps. **D** addresses.

_____ **6.** When you *transmit*, you
   A fix. **B** borrow. **C** send. **D** throw.

_____ **7.** Something that benefits *humankind* helps
   A your friends only. **C** your community only.
   B plants and animals. **D** people everywhere.

_____ **8.** Something that is an *impossibility* is
   A sure to happen. **B** likely to happen. **C** easy to do. **D** not possible.

_____ **9.** Countries known for their *closeness* on the map are
   A near each other. **B** far apart. **C** unfriendly. **D** the same size.

_____ **10.** When he *exceeded* the speed limit, he
   A obeyed it. **B** discussed it. **C** went beyond it. **D** went under it.

Word Skills

Writing

Even before the successful flight of the *Solar Challenger*, Paul MacCready had been experimenting with airplanes that were powered by alternative sources of energy. MacCready invented a bicycle-like plane that was powered by human energy and could be kept in the air by pedaling.

Write a letter requesting funding for an invention that harnesses an unusual energy source.

• What is the invention and how would it be operated?
• What source of energy does the invention use?
• What would be the benefits of your invention?

Be sure to use some of the vocabulary words from this unit in your writing.

_____

_____

_____

_____

_____

_____

_____

_____

_____

Writing

A Bridge to America

Read the selection. Think about the meanings of the **boldfaced** words. Then go back to the selection. Underline the words or sentences that give you a clue to the meaning of each **boldfaced** word.

When Columbus arrived in North America in 1492, he had made the journey by ship across a vast ocean. But many scientists believe that the first people who inhabited North America were able to walk here. How was this possible? After all, one look at a map will tell you that no other continent is **adjacent** to the Americas. The nearest land is the eastern end of Russia, and it is separated from Alaska by thirty-six miles of icy, arctic water.

However, we now know that this narrow **strait** in the Bering Sea was not always there. Fourteen thousand years ago, when the world was locked in an ice age, ice covered many of the northern **latitudes** of the globe. Because so much of Earth's water was frozen, the oceans shrank. So the land beneath what is now the Bering Sea was exposed. It formed a "land bridge" that linked the two continents and permitted the **forebears**, or ancestors, of today's Native Americans to walk to North America.

While no one can prove that **nomadic**, or wandering, tribes once traveled this path, scientists have **demonstrated** that the land bridge did exist. They know that the region was not always underwater because they have found fossils of land plants and animal bones in the Bering Sea. At one time, the Bering Sea was a vast grass-covered plain, inhabited by bison, horses, and giant mammoths.

The evidence for the land bridge makes it a **probable** route to North America. In addition, there is other strong evidence for the theory that the first Americans came from Asia. Racially, Asians are closely related to modern Native Americans. In addition, many Native American implements, customs, and legends resemble those of prehistoric Asians. Therefore, it seems likely that modern Native Americans are the **descendants** of prehistoric Asians.

One question still remains. Why did they come here? Since these early Asians were **migrants**, it seems possible that they might have accidentally wandered into North America in search of better hunting grounds. Whatever their reasons, they brought a new people and culture to a largely empty, **uninhabited** continent. Without this bridge to North America, the United States might be a very different place today.

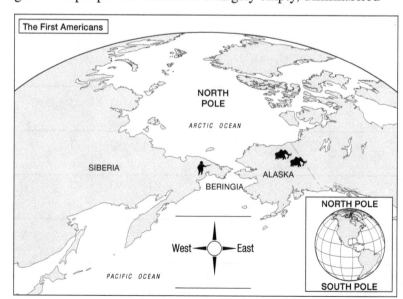

Context Clues

In each sentence a word or phrase is underlined. Use context clues from the selection to help you determine the meaning of the boxed words. Choose a word from the box to replace the underlined word or phrase in each sentence. Write the word on the line.

adjacent	demonstrated	descendants	forebears	latitudes
migrants	nomadic	probable	strait	uninhabited

1. According to many scientists, it is <u>reasonable to believe that</u> people from Asia crossed a land bridge and entered North America at least 12,000 years ago.

   _____

2. These people came from northeast Asia, the land <u>lying next</u> to what is modern-day Alaska.

   _____

3. These tribes were <u>constantly wandering</u> people who eventually moved south through areas of Canada into what is now the United States.

   _____

4. As they entered warmer <u>regions to the north or south of the equator</u>, there were major differences in the climate and natural surroundings.

   _____

5. These <u>roving people</u> saw plains and huge forests of spruce and fir.

   _____

6. These lands had been <u>not lived in</u> by people and were overflowing with animals, fish, and many different kinds of plants.

   _____

7. The <u>ancestors</u> of today's Native Americans became skillful hunters and fishers.

   _____

8. Like their <u>offspring who would come after them</u>, they respected the land around them and the animals living on it, and they took only what they needed to survive.

   _____

9. As they <u>proved by their actions</u>, they were prepared to meet the challenges of this new environment.

   _____

10. The wandering spirit of these Asian peoples had taken them far away from the <u>narrow channel connecting two larger bodies of water</u> that they first crossed to enter this new world.

   _____

Vocabulary in Context

Analogies

An analogy compares two pairs of words. The relationship between the first pair of words is the same as the relationship between the second pair of words. For example, *Finger* is to *hand* as *toe* is to *foot*. Use the words in the box to complete the following analogies.

adjacent	forebears	probable	strait	uninhabited

1. *Near* is to *far* as _____ is to *distant*.

2. *Pass* is to *mountains* as _____ is to *seas*.

3. *Clan* is to *family* as _____ is to *forefathers*.

4. *Complete* is to *finish* as _____ is to *likely*.

5. *Barren* is to *lush* as _____ is to *populated*.

Word Pairs

Words with similar parts may have related meanings. Study each word pair. Think about how the meanings of the words are alike. Check the meanings in the glossary. Then write a sentence for each word.

1. migrant—migration

_____

_____

2. demonstrate—demonstrative

_____

_____

3. nomad—nomadic

_____

_____

Name _____ Date _____

Word Game

The underlined letters in each sentence below appear in one of the words in the box. Use the underlined letters and the context of the sentence to determine the correct vocabulary word. Write the word on the line.

| adjacent | demonstrated | descendants | forebears | latitudes |
| migrants | nomadic | probable | strait | uninhabited |

1. The <u>ad</u> says there is a house right next to our store that is for <u>sa</u>le. _____

2. I know that <u>it</u> is possible to travel from the Atlantic Ocean to the Paci<u>fic</u> Ocean, but I cannot seem to find water linking the two seas on this map. _____

3. When you are <u>at</u> the equator, you know there are regions <u>to</u> the north and <u>to</u> the south that will have similar climates. _____

4. My great-grandparents used to see <u>bears</u> in the woods near our farm, but the animals have long since been frightened away by too many people. _____

5. I have a friend who gets <u>mad</u> whenever anyone suggests to her that she should settle <u>down</u> and stop wandering from city to city. _____

6. The singer cut a <u>demo</u> to show his singing style and try to prove to the record company that he had talent. _____

7. It's likely that no one could <u>rob</u> the house because extra locks were installed on all the doors and windows. _____

8. Many animals have ancestors that looked quite different from them, but it's hard to believe that <u>ants</u> ever looked any different than they do today. _____

9. It has become a <u>habit</u> with us to look for quiet beaches where we will not see <u>o</u>ther people. _____

10. The dogs <u>ran</u> from house to house, looking for a family that would <u>ta</u>ke them in. _____

Vocabulary in Context G9, SV 9780547625829

Crossword Puzzle

Use the words in the box and the clues to complete the crossword puzzle.

| adjacent | demonstrated | descendants | forebears | latitudes |
| migrants | nomadic | probable | strait | uninhabited |

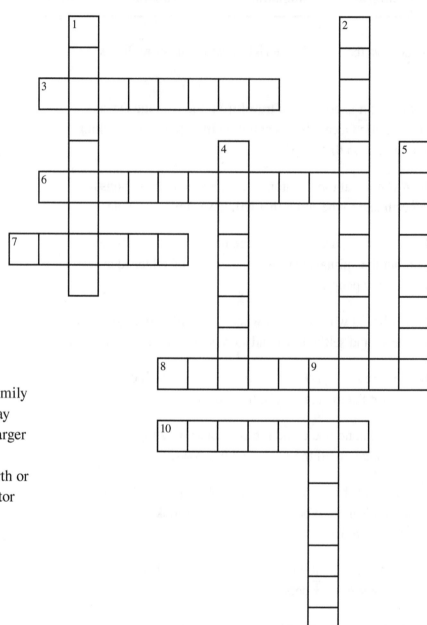

ACROSS

3. likely

6. people of a later generation of a family

7. a narrow waterway connecting two larger bodies of water

8. regions to the north or south of the equator

10. wandering

DOWN

1. ancestors

2. showed

4. nearby

5. people who move from place to place

9. not lived in

Standardized Test Practice

Circle the letter of the word that best completes the sentence.

Vocabulary in Context

> **TIP**
>
> Read carefully. Use the other words in the sentence to help you choose the missing word.

1. The _____ of today's Native Americans were adventurers.

   A travelers   **B** forebears   **C** hunters   **D** nomadic

2. The musicians _____ their talent with a wonderful performance.

   A showing   **B** sang   **C** demonstrated   **D** uninhabited

3. Farmworkers who travel from place to place for work are called _____.

   A latitudes   **B** picking   **C** keepers   **D** migrants

4. As far as scientists know, nearby planets are _____ by people.

   A uninhabited   **B** demonstrated   **C** worked   **D** auctioned

5. The family crossed the _____ in a large sailboat.

   A desert   **B** uninhabited   **C** hills   **D** strait

6. There are _____ cultures around the world whose wandering ways make their lives very different from the lives of people who live in the same place for much of their lives.

   A descendants   **B** move   **C** nomadic   **D** forebears

7. Countries that are located in the _____ near the equator have a warm climate.

   A migrants   **B** latitudes   **C** adjacent   **D** poles

8. It is very _____ that the dog came looking for a biscuit.

   A probable   **B** uninhabited   **C** migrants   **D** adjacent

9. The Wongs bought the house _____ to ours.

   A probable   **B** adjacent   **C** strait   **D** distance

10. Their _____ still live in the same part of the world.

    A descendants   **B** wandering   **C** demonstrated   **D** relationships

Understanding Related Words

The words in the box can be related to the theme of construction. See how many of these words you already know. Use the glossary to find definitions of unfamiliar words.

airtight	bedrock	casualties	comprises	density
excavation	immersed	impervious	laborious	productive

Write each word from the box next to its meaning.

1. _____ : the process of digging, hollowing out, or removing

2. _____ : injuries or deaths

3. _____ : solid rock just below Earth's surface

4. _____ : consists of; includes

5. _____ : thickness; compactness

6. _____ : not allowing air to come in or go out

7. _____ : not capable of being penetrated

8. _____ : completely covered by a liquid

9. _____ : requiring long, hard work

10. _____ : effective

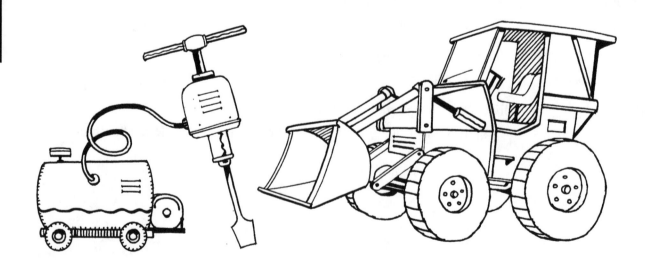

Word Skills

Synonyms and Antonyms

Synonyms are words that have similar meanings, while antonyms are words that have opposite meanings.
Look at the words below. If they are synonyms, put a (✓) in the Synonyms column. If they are antonyms,
put a (✓) in the Antonyms column.

	Antonyms	Synonyms
1. airtight—leaky	_____	_____
2. casualties—injuries	_____	_____
3. productive—ineffective	_____	_____
4. immersed—submerged	_____	_____
5. impervious—penetrable	_____	_____

Dictionary Skills

Each item below has two parts. Answer the first part by writing a word from the box. Answer
the second part by circling the correct choice. Use the pronunciation key in a dictionary to help you
when necessary.

bedrock	comprises	density	excavation	laborious

1. Write the correct spelling of kəm prīz´iz. _____
   It means   **a.** is composed of.   **b.** rewards worth working for.

2. Write the correct spelling of eks´kə vā´shən. _____
   It means   **a.** the act of digging.   **b.** the process of caving in.

3. Write the correct spelling of den´si tē. _____
   It means   **a.** how far from home.   **b.** how closely packed together.

4. Write the correct spelling of lə bôr´ē əs. _____
   It means   **a.** clearing out or deepening.   **b.** involving hard work.

5. Write the correct spelling of bed´rok´. _____
   It means   **a.** rock found along riverbeds. **b.** solid stone under Earth's surface.

Unit 3
Vocabulary in Context G9, SV 9780547625829

Word Skills

Completing Sentences

Write the letter of the word or phrase that completes each sentence.

_____ 1. If a bookcase *comprises* three shelves, the three shelves are what it is
     A made of.   B used for.   C on top of.   D sometimes called.

_____ 2. A *productive* person is
     A slow.   B violent.   C effective.   D effortless.

_____ 3. When something is *immersed* in water, it is
     A dried.   B submerged.   C sprinkled.   D dampened.

_____ 4. *Casualties* in war are soldiers and others who are
     A trained.   B brave.   C lucky.   D wounded.

_____ 5. When you hit *bedrock*, you are on
     A loose soil.   B a mountain.   C solid rock.   D the moon.

_____ 6. The *density* of an object can be measured by its
     A parts.   B movements.   C appearance.   D compactness.

_____ 7. A bottle that is *airtight* is
     A securely shut.   B wide open.   C small.   D empty.

_____ 8. A *laborious* job is one that is
     A temporary.   B permanent.   C easy.   D difficult.

_____ 9. A covering that is *impervious* to water is
     A sturdy.   B flimsy.   C waterproof.   D saturated.

_____ 10. An *excavation* may turn up something that is
     A in a building.   B underground.   C on a hilltop.   D in the air.

Writing

Imagine what it would be like to live on a remote, uninhabited island. You would have to create everything you need to survive.

In one or two paragraphs, write about your life there.

• Which things that you use every day would be unavailable to you in such a place?
  What might you use instead?
• What would you do for fun?
• Where would you get food, clothing, and shelter?

Be sure to use some of the vocabulary words from this unit in your writing.

_____

_____

_____

_____

_____

_____

_____

_____

_____

Writing

The Cajuns

by Howard Peet

Read the selection. Think about the meanings of the **boldfaced** words. Then go back to the selection. Underline the words or sentences that give you a clue to the meaning of each **boldfaced** word.

The Cajuns are a group of people who live mainly in southern Louisiana. They are descendants of the Acadians, French settlers who, in the 1600s and early 1700s, lived in southeastern Canada. This selection tells the unusual history of this group.

> This is the forest primeval[1]; but where are the hearts that beneath it
> Leaped like the roe,[2] when he hears in the woodland the voice of the huntsman?
> Where is the thatch-roofed village, the home of Acadian farmers,—
> —Henry Wadsworth Longfellow

In Henry Wadsworth Longfellow's poem *Evangeline*, the history of the Cajun culture unfolds in a moving tale of love and loyalty. Cajun history begins in the region that now includes Nova Scotia, New Brunswick, Prince Edward Island, parts of Quebec, and parts of Maine. The French settlers of this area called it Acadia. At first, they lived happily and well. The land produced a **bounteous** harvest, and the farms were **profitable**. The sea, the forests, and the mountains were breathtaking in their beauty. There were no taxes or government **tariffs** to drain the wealth of the people. The Acadians, an **unpretentious** folk who enjoyed a simple existence, **prospered**.

However, both France and Great Britain claimed this region as their own. In 1713, the Treaty of Utrecht gave Acadia to Britain. The British were **jubilant**, of course, but the Acadians were not. They were not a **belligerent**, or warlike, people; they did not openly rebel when British rule became **operative**. They did, however, **sympathize** with France, their native country. Their attitude, expressed in **contemptuous quips** about the new British king and his rule, did not **endear** the Acadians to their British neighbors—or to King George I.

In the years that followed, war between Britain and France in North America seemed more and more likely. The British were afraid that the Acadians would **revert** to their French loyalties in wartime. So, in 1755, all Acadians who refused to take an oath of allegiance to the King of Great Britain were **deported**. People sympathetic to the Acadians have always argued that nothing the Acadians had done **warranted** such severe treatment. Nonetheless, they were forced to leave behind their land, homes, and most of their possessions. They were allowed to carry only a few personal **mementos** with them.

It was a tragic time for the Acadians. They were scattered in a **random** pattern among British colonies to the south. Many of them drifted into the deep southern United States. For some time they **floundered** in their efforts to keep their identity, but they held onto their close feelings toward one another. Finally, a community of Acadians began to form again. Its **nucleus** was near the Mississippi River Delta.

---

[1] primeval: belonging to the first ages of the world

[2] roe: a small deer

Longfellow's poem tells the story of two Acadians, Evangeline and Gabriel, who were separated during this forced move. Evangeline's lifelong search for Gabriel represents the Acadians' search for their lost home. In fact, Evangeline's kind of loyalty became one of the highest values in the culture.

The Acadians, now called the Cajuns, keep the memory of Evangeline and the tradition of the old days alive. Under the big Evangeline Oak in St. Martinville, Louisiana, is a plaque. The plaque, which bears the names of the real-life Evangeline and Gabriel, stands as a **belated** recognition of their devotion.

Name _____   Date _____

Context Clues

Write the meaning of the word or phrase that is closest in meaning to the word or words in italics. Use context clues to help you choose the correct answer.

_____ 1. Since Elodia's birthday was last week, the birthday party we are having for her this evening is *belated*.

    A preliminary   **B** surprising   **C** exclusive   **D** late

_____ 2. With someone as *belligerent* as Tom around, arguments break out all the time.

    A quarrelsome   **B** delicate   **C** friendly   **D** diligent

_____ 3. A *bounteous* meal filled the tables to overflowing at Thanksgiving.

    A more than sufficient   **C** plain and healthful

    B thrifty   **D** grave

_____ 4. Catherine insisted she was not *contemptuous* of the television show we chose, but she sneered and made fun of it all the time we were watching.

    A proud   **B** scornful   **C** fearful   **D** respectful

_____ 5. A British person who is *deported from* the United States would most likely return to Britain.

    A sent out of   **B** brought into   **C** imprisoned in   **D** accused in

_____ 6. Mary's appealing ways *endear her* to everyone who meets her.

    A make her different from   **C** make her devoted to

    B make her liked by   **D** make her more energetic than

_____ 7. Trying to get out of the swamp, Ben *floundered*, almost falling, and eventually had to call for help.

    A swam   **B** hesitated   **C** struggled   **D** proposed

_____ 8. The whole school was *jubilant* when our team won the tournament.

    A passive   **B** effective   **C** tired   **D** joyful

_____ 9. When we moved, I kept a rock from the backyard as a *memento* of our first house.

    A reminder   **B** vagabond   **C** picture   **D** description

_____ 10. The *nucleus* of our city is the downtown area; everything else surrounds it.

    A exterior   **B** habitat   **C** diameter   **D** central part

_____ **11.** The new student code of behavior will be *operative* November 15. From that day on, all students will be expected to obey the new rules.

    A wrong   **B** in effect   **C** realistic   **D** exciting

_____ **12.** Babysitting every weekend must be *profitable* for Jerome. I just saw him in a new jacket.

    A tiring   **B** offensive   **C** moneymaking   **D** difficult

_____ **13.** Many people hope that if they get a good job and work hard, they will *prosper.*

    A do well   **B** get by   **C** leave soon   **D** dream

_____ **14.** People on television are always trading *quips*, but I can never think of anything funny to say until it's too late.

    A appointments   **B** gestures   **C** clever remarks   **D** strange responses

_____ **15.** The students took *random* seats in the classroom rather than using a seating chart.

    A unplanned   **B** careful   **C** hurried   **D** confusing

_____ **16.** As oil becomes scarcer, we may have to *revert to* sources of energy used more commonly years ago, such as coal and wood.

    A give up   **B** invent   **C** go back to   **D** waste

_____ **17.** Aesha *sympathized with* the Johnsons' problems, so she offered to help.

    A was annoyed by   **B** understood   **C** believed   **D** envied

_____ **18.** The *tariffs* that a government places on goods that come into a country increase the price of the goods.

    A seals   **B** taxes   **C** discounts   **D** guards

_____ **19.** Although her family is one of the richest and most powerful in our town, Isabel is an *unpretentious* person.

    A arrogant   **B** proud   **C** modest   **D** responsive

_____ **20.** Danny knew he was wrong, but he didn't think his mistake *warranted* the harsh punishment he received.

    A prevented   **B** erased   **C** affected   **D** justified

Vocabulary in Context

Name _____ Date _____

Matching Ideas

Write the word from the box that is most clearly related to the situation described in the sentences or groups of sentences.

| deported | floundered | memento | prosper | random |

1. Walking across a field, Hector suddenly stepped in a muddy area. Caught by surprise, he kicked and stumbled, trying to get to the other side.

    _____

2. The young child was told to select one gift from the pile. She could not decide which one to choose, so she closed her eyes and took the first one she touched.

    _____

3. The detectives caught the foreign criminal. She was arrested and was soon sent back to her native country.

    _____

4. The online business is so successful that many new customers sign up each week and sales increase daily.

    _____

5. Aiko keeps a box on the shelf of her closet and into it she puts old letters, special photographs, and other souvenirs.

    _____

True-False

Decide whether each statement is true (T) or false (F). Write *T* or *F* for each statement.

_____ 1. If your business is *profitable*, you will probably be forced to close it soon.

_____ 2. An *unpretentious* person usually brags a lot.

_____ 3. A *belated* award is given some time after the achievement.

_____ 4. A *contemptuous* person shows respect for others.

_____ 5. A person who *reverts* to the behavior of childhood might throw food.

_____ 6. If a harvest is *bounteous*, the farmer will probably make a great deal of money that year.

_____ 7. If your furnace is *operative*, it can keep your house warm.

_____ 8. A grandmother would not want to spend the afternoon with a grandson who has *endeared* himself to her.

_____ 9. If you are *deported*, you do not go to another country.

_____ 10. Warmhearted people *sympathize* easily with others.

Unit 4
Vocabulary in Context G9, SV 9780547625829

Vocabulary in Context

Name _____ Date _____

Standardized Test Practice

Circle the letter of the word that is a synonym of the capitalized word.

> **TIP**
> Remember to read all of the answer choices. If you do not know which one is correct, mark out the ones you are sure are incorrect and choose from the ones that are left.

1. BELLIGERENT

   A peaceful   **C** warlike

   B diligent   **D** polite

2. JUBILANT

   A curious   **C** wistful

   B joyous   **D** brisk

3. NUCLEUS

   A center   **C** bomb

   B rim   **D** factor

4. QUIP

   A wisecrack   **C** ending

   B dream   **D** strike

5. TARIFF

   A fight   **C** tax

   B emotion   **D** attitude

6. WARRANTED

   A offended   **C** arrested

   B complimented   **D** justified

Circle the letter of the word that is an antonym of the capitalized word.

7. BELATED

   A delayed   **B** prompt   **C** discussed   **D** confused

8. BOUNTEOUS

   A huge   **B** sparse   **C** ugly   **D** bumpy

9. CONTEMPTUOUS

   A scornful   **B** modern   **C** admiring   **D** daring

Circle the letter of the word or words that best complete the sentence.

10. If the children *endear* themselves to their babysitter, she will

    A adore them.   **B** neglect them.   **C** feed them.   **D** put them to bed early.

11. If a student *floundered* at learning a new language, he would most likely

    A get an *A* in French class.   **C** skip to the next level in Spanish class.

    B not do very well in German class.   **D** study many different languages.

12. If your principal told you students had to *revert* to a different system, it would most likely be

    A a new one.   **B** an old one.   **C** a better one.   **D** an unusual one.

    Vocabulary in Context G9, SV 9780547625829

Understanding Related Words

The words in the box are closely related to the vocabulary words. See how many of the words you already know. Use the glossary to find definitions of unfamiliar words.

sympathy	warranty	pretense	profit	jubilant
sympathized	warrants	pretentious	profitable	jubilee

Use one of these pairs of closely related words in the box to complete each sentence below. Write the correct word on each line. Use the glossary to find the meaning of any word you do not know.

1. Ms. Lonnigan sells her merchandise at the lowest price in town. She makes very little

   _____ on each sale, but because she sells so much, her business is

   _____.

2. Alicia is _____ about performing in the _____, which

   celebrates the fiftieth anniversary of the town's founding.

3. Donald is a very _____ person. His brother, on the other hand, shows no

   _____, even though he comes from the same famous family.

4. I _____ with Lemar when his grandfather died recently, so I sent him a

   _____ card.

5. This car will be very expensive to repair, and I think that _____ paying the

   extra fee to extend the _____.

Dictionary Skills

Without using a dictionary, divide each of the following words into syllables, inserting a hyphen between syllables. Be sure that the division of each word includes all the letters of the word. When you have finished, use a dictionary to check your work.

1. sympathized _____

2. jubilee _____

3. warranty _____

4. pretentious _____

5. belligerent _____

6. contemptuous _____

Word Skills

The Latin Root *vert*

The word *revert* comes from the Latin word *vertere*, meaning "to turn." The following words all come from this same Latin word.

convert	divert	invert	reverse	controversy

Keeping in mind the meaning of *vertere*, write each related word from the box beside its correct definition. Use the glossary if necessary.

_____ **1.** turn upside down

_____ **2.** change from one form or belief to another; exchange for something equal in value

_____ **3.** turn backward

_____ **4.** a discussion in which people oppose each other

_____ **5.** turn aside

Challenge Yourself

1. Name two things you could do to make a <u>profit</u>.

_____

2. Name two times when you have felt <u>sympathy</u>.

_____

3. Name two things for which you might get a <u>warranty</u>.

_____

Word Pairs

As you read each pair of words, think about how they are alike. Write the word from the box that best completes each group.

controversy	pretense	profit	sympathy	warranty

1. earnings, income, _____

2. argument, disagreement, _____

3. kindness, compassion, _____

4. guarantee, contract, _____

5. make-believe, affectation, _____

Forming Words

Using the letters found in the word *pretentious*, make ten words of four or more letters. For example, the word *soup* can be formed using the letters in *pretentious*.

1. _____   6. _____

2. _____   7. _____

3. _____   8. _____

4. _____   9. _____

5. _____   10. _____

Vocabulary in Context G9, SV 9780547625829

Word Skills

Writing

The reading selection tells about the loyalty of the Cajuns. Write a paragraph telling what you think loyalty is and why it is important.

• Is loyalty profitable?
• Does it help people to prosper?
• Does it endear people to each other?
• What are some examples of loyalty? When might loyalty *not* be appropriate?

Use some vocabulary words from this unit in your writing.

_____

_____

_____

_____

_____

_____

_____

_____

_____

_____

Writing

Statues That Wait

Read the selection. Think about the meanings of the **boldfaced** words. Then go back to the selection. Underline the words or sentences that give you a clue to the meaning of each **boldfaced** word.

Easter Island is **situated** 2,400 miles west of Chile, in the South Pacific Ocean. Geographically, there is nothing unusual about this island, yet it is one of the most famous islands in the world. The Dutch were the first to **colonize** Easter Island, bringing settlers from Europe in 1722. They were also the first Westerners to see the remarkable sight that has amazed people for over 250 years.

They found a series of fascinating sculptures—more than six hundred of them—scattered over the island. Some of the sculptures were carved in the shape of long, thin faces with no eyes. The sculptures have long ears, jutting chins, and tiny legs. The sculptures' only **adornments** are around their stomachs. It took incredible skill and **artistry** to create the statues. This is evident in the careful carving and precise placement of one stone on top of another. Some of the statues had red stone cylinders balanced on their enormous heads like hats, but all of these have long ago fallen off. Experts who have studied the statues believe their creators carved them with hand picks out of rock from an extinct volcano on the island.

Some of these **monumental** statues stand as tall as a three-story house and weigh over fifty tons. Many people find it **incomprehensible** that a primitive society could have moved such huge, bulky, **cumbersome** stones and put them into place facing the ocean.

Others have looked for an answer to why the mysterious statues were built in the first place. Were they meant to represent something, or have a **symbolic** purpose? One theory claims they were made to **commemorate**, or honor the memory of, the builders' ancestors. Another theory points to the fact that the statues look out to the ocean, as though they were waiting for something. Perhaps the statues were meant to form a **citadel**, or fort, to protect the islands against a hostile attack from the sea. A French writer who visited the island in 1870 put it best when he wrote, "They have no eyes, only deep cavities under their large, noble foreheads, yet they seem to be looking and thinking. . . ."

Context Clues

In each sentence a word or phrase is underlined. Choose a word from the box to replace that word or phrase. Write the word on the line.

adornments	artistry	citadel	colonize	commemorate
cumbersome	incomprehensible	monumental	situated	symbolic

1. The statues of Easter Island surround the island like a protective <u>fort</u>. _____

2. The statues were <u>placed</u> so they would look out to the ocean. _____

3. The <u>skillful work of the artists</u> used to carve the faces is evident in all of the monuments. _____

4. Since the Dutch were the first to <u>settle</u> Easter Island, they were the first Westerners to see the statues. _____

5. Visitors are awed that the people of Easter Island were able to move the large stones that were <u>clumsy and difficult to manage</u>. _____

6. Today, the <u>massive</u> statues draw visitors from around the world. _____

7. Did these statues have a <u>representative</u> and special purpose for the ancient people of this place? _____

8. Many experts who study the statues find it <u>unbelievable</u> that a primitive society could move such heavy objects. _____

9. Perhaps the carving on the statues is there to <u>pay honor</u> to the builders' ancestors who first populated Easter Island. _____

10. The stone giants have <u>decorations</u> only around their stomachs. _____

Understanding Multiple-Meaning Words

The words in the box have more than one meaning. Look for context clues in each sentence to tell which meaning is being used. Write the letter of the correct meaning next to the sentence.

monumental
a. huge or enormous in size
b. very important

_____ **1.** The pyramids of Egypt, like the statues of Easter Island, are <u>monumental</u> structures that rise high above the ground.

_____ **2.** The discovery of the statues on Easter Island was <u>monumental</u> for those Westerners who study ancient cultures.

citadel
a. fort
b. safe place

_____ **3.** After the earthquake, the church became a <u>citadel</u> for those people forced out from their homes.

_____ **4.** The <u>citadel</u> that housed the soldiers was made of heavy stones.

Word Groups

As you read each pair of words, think about how they are alike. Write the word from the box that best completes each group.

adornments	artistry	citadel	colonize	commemorate
cumbersome	incomprehensible	monumental	situate	symbolic

1. settle, establish, _____

2. craft, skill, _____

3. unbelievable, incredible,

_____

4. bulky, awkward, _____

5. representative, meaningful,

_____

6. honor, remember, _____

7. decorations, ornaments,

_____

8. fort, refuge, _____

9. gigantic, massive, _____

10. place, locate, _____

Word Map

Use the words in the box to complete the word map about the statues of Easter Island. Add other words that you know to each category.

adornments	artistry	citadel	commemorate
cumbersome	incomprehensible	monumental	symbolic

What We See

1. _____

2. _____

3. _____

4. _____

5. _____

Purpose of the Statues

1. _____

2. _____

3. _____

4. _____

5. _____

EASTER ISLAND STATUES

Reactions to the Statues

1. _____

2. _____

3. _____

4. _____

5. _____

Synonyms and Antonyms

Synonyms are words that have similar meanings, while antonyms are words that have opposite meanings. Look at the words below. If they are synonyms, put a (✓) in the Synonyms column. If they are antonyms, put a (✓) in the Antonyms column.

	Antonyms	Synonyms
1. commemorate—ignore	_____	_____
2. citadel—fortress	_____	_____
3. incomprehensible—understandable	_____	_____
4. monumental—unimportant	_____	_____
5. artistry—talent	_____	_____

The Suffixes -able and -ible

The suffixes -able and -ible mean "able to be." When these suffixes are added to a base word or root, they create adjectives. Add -able or -ible to these nouns to create adjectives. Note that sometimes the end of the noun will change before adding the suffix. Use a dictionary for spelling if needed.

1. note: _____

2. laugh: _____

3. sense: _____

4. permission: _____

5. reuse: _____

6. excuse: _____

7. comfort: _____

8. permit: _____

9. adjust: _____

10. deduct: _____

Standardized Test Practice

Circle the letter of the word or words that best complete the sentence.

TIP

Read each sentence carefully. Then read all of the answer choices. Many choices may make sense, but only one choice has the same or almost the same meaning as the italicized word.

1. To *colonize* is to

   A commemorate.   **B** destroy.   **C** settle.   **D** avoid.

2. People are protected in a *citadel*, which is a

   A machine.   **B** potion.   **C** navy.   **D** fort.

3. If something is *incomprehensible*, it is

   A interesting.   **B** massive.   **C** upside-down.   **D** unbelievable.

4. Things with *adornments* on them are

   A ancient.   **B** decorated.   **C** awkward.   **D** full.

5. If you know where something is *situated*, then you know where it is

   A honored.   **B** located.   **C** decorated.   **D** managed.

6. Carrying a *cumbersome* box is

   A exciting.   **B** simple.   **C** awkward.   **D** symbolic.

7. To *commemorate* means to

   A meet.   **B** honor.   **C** trust.   **D** talk to.

8. A building that is *monumental* is

   A enormous.   **B** ordinary.   **C** attractive.   **D** artistic.

9. A *symbolic* object is used to

   A destroy.   **B** colonize.   **C** represent.   **D** reverse.

10. The *artistry* of that design shows

    A craziness.   **B** broken tools.   **C** skillful work.   **D** lazy work.

Vocabulary in Context

Understanding Related Words

The words in the box can be related to building monuments. See how many of the words you already know. Use the glossary to find definitions of unfamiliar words.

architecture	authorized	completion	creativity	dignifies
eligible	heroism	immortality	milestone	veterans

Write each word from the box in front of its meaning.

1. _____ : makes noble or worthy

2. _____ : condition of being finished

3. _____ : those who have served in the armed forces

4. _____ : bravery, especially in a dangerous situation

5. _____ : the state of living forever

6. _____ : the planning and designing of buildings

7. _____ : gave power to

8. _____ : an important event

9. _____ : qualified; fit to be chosen

10. _____ : imagination; the ability to invent or design

Word Skills

Word Groups

As you read each pair of words, think about how they are alike. Write the word from the box that best completes each group.

architecture	authorized	creativity	dignifies
eligible	heroism	milestone	veterans

1. bravery, courage, _____

2. enabled, allowed, _____

3. soldiers, sailors, _____

4. respects, honors, _____

5. suitable, acceptable, _____

6. cleverness, imagination, _____

7. building, design, _____

8. landmark, celebration, _____

Word Pairs

Words with similar parts may have related meanings. Study each word pair. Think about how the meanings are alike. Check the meanings in the glossary. Then write a sentence for each word.

1. creation—creativity

_____

_____

2. heroic—heroism

_____

_____

3. dignity—dignifies

_____

_____

4. authorized—authorization

_____

_____

Word Skills

Synonyms

Choose the word that is a synonym for the capitalized word. Write the letter of the word on the line.

_____   **1.** HEROISM

        A speed   **B** bravery   **C** luck   **D** humor

_____   **2.** DIGNIFIES

        A illustrates   **B** aids   **C** understands   **D** honors

_____   **3.** COMPLETION

        A finishing   **B** idea   **C** category   **D** organization

_____   **4.** MILESTONE

        A fortune   **B** help   **C** event   **D** intelligence

_____   **5.** IMMORTALITY

        A knowledge   **B** interest   **C** pure goodness   **D** everlasting life

_____   **6.** ELIGIBLE

        A attractive   **B** qualified   **C** harmless   **D** ignorant

_____   **7.** ARCHITECTURE

        A design   **B** politics   **C** decoration   **D** value

_____   **8.** VETERANS

        A musicians   **B** floats   **C** former soldiers   **D** animal doctors

_____   **9.** AUTHORIZED

        A welcomed   **B** gave ideas to   **C** placed blame on   **D** gave power to

_____   **10.** CREATIVITY

        A imagination   **B** loneliness   **C** jealousy   **D** dishonesty

Word Skills

Writing

Write about a monument you would create to honor a person or people who have showed heroism.

- What does the monument look like? Does it have adornments?
- Which person or people does your monument dignify? Describe the heroism of this person or these people.

Use some vocabulary words from this unit in your writing.

_____

_____

_____

_____

_____

_____

_____

_____

_____

_____

_____

_____

Writing

All Gold Canyon

by Jack London

Read the selection. Think about the meanings of the **boldfaced** words. Then go back to the selection. Underline the words or sentences that give you a clue to the meaning of each **boldfaced** word.

In the following selection, Jack London uses colorful descriptive language to paint an appealing picture. He describes a place of great peace and beauty.

It was the green heart of the canyon, where the walls swerved back from the **rigid** plain and relieved their harshness of line by making a little sheltered nook and filling it to the brim with sweetness and roundness and softness. Here all things rested. Even the narrow stream **ceased** its **turbulent** down-rush long enough to form a quiet pool. Knee-deep in the water, with drooping head and half-shut eyes, drowsed a red-coated, many-antlered buck.

On one side, beginning at the very lip of the pool, was a tiny meadow, a cool **resilient** surface of green that extended to the base of the frowning wall. Beyond the pool a gentle slope of earth ran up and up to meet the opposing wall. Fine grass covered the slope—grass that was spangled with flowers, with here and there patches of color, orange and purple and golden. Below, the canyon was shut in. There was no view. The walls leaned together **abruptly**, and the canyon ended in a **chaos** of rocks, moss-covered and hidden by a green screen of vines and creepers and boughs of trees. Up the canyon rose far hills and peaks, the big foothills, pine-covered and **remote**. And far beyond, like clouds upon the border of the sky, towered minarets[1] of white, where the Sierra's eternal snows flashed **austerely** the blazes of the sun.

There was no dust in the canyon. The leaves and flowers were clean and virginal.[2] The grass was young velvet. Over the pool three cottonwoods sent their snowy fluffs fluttering down the quiet air. On the slope the blossoms of the wine-wooded manzanita[3] filled the air with springtime odors, while the leaves, wise with experience, were already beginning their **vertical** twist against the coming **aridity** of summer. In the open spaces on the slope, beyond the farthest shadow-reach of the manzanita, **poised** the mariposa lilies, like so many flights of jeweled moths suddenly **arrested** and on the **verge** of trembling into flight again.

Here and there that woods harlequin,[4] the madrone,[5] permitting itself to be caught in the act of changing its pea-green trunk to madder-red,[6] breathed its fragrance into the air from great clusters of waxen bells. Creamy white were these bells, shaped like lilies of the valley, with the sweetness of perfume that is of the springtime.

There was not a sigh of wind. The air was drowsy with its weight of perfume. It was a sweetness that would have been cloying[7] had the air been heavy and humid. But the air was sharp and thin. It was as starlight transmuted[8] into atmosphere, shot through and warmed by sunshine, and flower-drenched with sweetness.

An occasional butterfly drifted in and out through the patches of light and shade. And from all about rose the low and sleepy hum of mountain bees—feasting Sybarites[9] that **jostled** one another good-naturedly at the board, nor found time for rough discourtesy. So quietly did the little stream drip and ripple its way through the canyon that it spoke only in faint and occasional gurgles. The voice of the stream was as a drowsy whisper, ever interrupted by dozings and silences, ever lifted again in the awakenings.

The motion of all things was a drifting in the heart of the canyon. Sunshine and butterflies drifted in and out among the trees. The hum of the bees and the whisper of the stream were a drifting of sound. And the drifting sound and drifting color seemed to weave together in the making of a delicate and **intangible** fabric which was the **spirit** of the place. It was a spirit of peace that was not of death, but of smooth-pulsing life, of **quietude** that was not silence, of movement that was not action, of **repose** that was quick with existence without being violent with struggle and **travail**. The spirit of the place was the spirit of the peace of the living, **somnolent** with the easement[10] and content of prosperity, and undisturbed by rumors of far wars.

[1]minarets: towers on mosques, Moslem places of worship
[2]virginal: pure; fresh
[3]manzanita: shrub or small tree found in the western United States
[4]harlequin: a playful clown from Italian drama
[5]madrone: evergreen tree of western North America
[6]madder-red: a bright, orangy red
[7]cloying: too sweet or rich
[8]transmuted: changed from one form to another
[9]Sybarites: citizens of an ancient Greek city who prized luxury
[10]easement: comfort; relief

Vocabulary in Context G9, SV 9780547625829

Context Clues

Write the letter of the word or phrase that is closest in meaning to the word or words in italics. Use context clues to help you choose the correct answer.

_____ **1.** The car bounced when the road changed *abruptly* from blacktop to gravel.

    A gradually   **B** smoothly   **C** suddenly   **D** carefully

_____ **2.** Rain forests are dense and damp, while deserts are known for their emptiness and *aridity*.

    A size   **B** toxin   **C** condition   **D** dryness

_____ **3.** The statue of the running horse was so realistic that it looked as though a real animal had been *arrested* in mid-gallop.

    A tripped   **B** ticketed   **C** brushed   **D** stopped

_____ **4.** With little time or money for luxuries, most pioneers lived *austerely* in sod houses or log cabins.

    A wastefully   **B** comfortably   **C** plainly   **D** joyfully

_____ **5.** The moment after the music *ceased*, it seemed as though we could still hear it.

    A stopped   **B** became quieter   **C** increased   **D** began

_____ **6.** Aisha's room was as neat as a pin, but in Tamika's room there was total *chaos*.

    A lack of order   **B** loud noise   **C** happiness   **D** calm

_____ **7.** Besides food, shelter, and other objects, human beings seem to need such *intangible* things as love to really be happy.

    A physical   **B** painful   **C** cheerful   **D** nonmaterial

_____ **8.** The people in the crowd were basically happy and well-behaved, only *jostling* one another a little and kidding the ticket takers.

    A helping   **B** slugging   **C** pursuing   **D** bumping

_____ **9.** The huge boulder was *poised* at the edge of the cliff as if at any moment it might topple off.

    A buried   **B** balanced   **C** shoved   **D** unloaded

_____ **10.** Having escaped the noise of the busy city, we enjoyed the *quietude* of our uncle's farm.

    A activity   **B** peace   **C** richness   **D** luxuriousness

_____ **11.** Many people would be unhappy at the ranger station because it is so far away from civilization. Dakota, on the other hand, loves it because it is so *remote*.

    A high   **B** distant   **C** busy   **D** beautiful

_____ **12.** David, sitting against a tree and holding a fishing pole, enjoyed his *repose* on the sunny side of the riverbank.

    A exercise   **B** burrow   **C** rest   **D** job

_____ **13.** After the storm the grass sprang back tall and straight, *resilient* as the string of an archer's bow.

    A recovering its shape quickly   **C** unusually long

    B weak and droopy   **D** sleek and lovely

_____ **14.** When spaghetti is boiled, it becomes limp. However, when it is dry, spaghetti is completely *rigid*.

    A tasteless   **B** bad-tasting   **C** stiff   **D** slimy

_____ **15.** Even though I was sitting up, the motion of the train made me so *somnolent* I had trouble staying awake.

    A sleepy   **B** sick   **C** nervous   **D** uncomfortable

_____ **16.** Because of the people who work there, that office has such a *spirit* of fun and friendliness that few employees leave for other jobs.

    A habitat   **B** responsibility   **C** mood   **D** ghost

_____ **17.** Though many of today's job situations are difficult, few people can imagine the *travail* of those who, a hundred years ago, had to work sixteen to eighteen hours each day.

    A scars   **B** profit   **C** hard labor   **D** huge debts

_____ **18.** As the storm clouds gathered and then unleashed rain while thunder roared, many old-timers said they had never seen weather more *turbulent*.

    A brisk   **B** rough   **C** mild   **D** sudden

_____ **19.** As he felt the anger rising inside him, Kevin realized he was *on the verge of* losing his temper.

    A very close to   **B** far from   **C** afraid of   **D** deliberately

_____ **20.** The supports the carpenter put up were *vertical*, reaching from the floor to the ceiling.

    A upright   **B** crooked   **C** metal   **D** sideways

    Vocabulary in Context G9, SV 9780547625829

Using Context Clues

Reread the selection on pages 58–59. For each of the following items, consider how the vocabulary word is used in the selection. Write the letter of the word or phrase that best completes the sentence.

_____ **1.** By using *resilient* to describe the meadow, the author suggests
  A soft and healthy.   **B** cool and damp.   **C** new and fragile.

_____ **2.** The "*chaos* of rocks" in which the canyon ends is most likely
  A a stone wall.   **B** a heap of boulders.   **C** a deep pit.

_____ **3.** Within the context of the selection, *arrested* suggests moths that are
  A flying quickly.   **B** hurt.   **C** frozen in mid-flight.

_____ **4.** The word *travail* in the last paragraph of the selection suggests work that is
  A easy and rewarding.   **B** painfully difficult.   **C** challenging.

_____ **5.** By saying that the spirit of the place is *somnolent*, the author suggests
  A brightness.   **B** effortlessness.   **C** hopelessness.

Figures of Speech

Writers use **figures of speech** to add interest to their writing. **Personification** is a figure of speech that gives human characteristics to an animal or a thing. **Similes** and **metaphors** are figures of speech that compare two unlike things. Similes make comparisons using the words *like* or *as*.

Decide whether each underlined statement is an example of personification, simile, or metaphor. Write the correct answer on the line.

1. On one side, beginning at the very lip of the pool, was a tiny meadow, a cool resilient surface of green that extended to the base of the frowning wall.   _____

2. And far beyond, like clouds upon the border of the sky, towered minarets of white, where the Sierra's eternal snows flashed austerely the blazes of the sun.   _____

3. The grass was young velvet.   _____

4. On the slope the blossoms of the wine-wooded manzanita filled the air with springtime odors, while the leaves, wise with experience, were already beginning their vertical twist against the coming aridity of summer.   _____

Name _____ Date _____

Standardized Test Practice

Determine the relationship between the pair of capitalized words. Then decide which other word pair expresses a similar relationship. Circle the letter of the correct pair.

 TIP

When reading analogies, remember to figure out the relationship between the first two words before you look for the correct answer.

1. QUIETUDE : PEACE : :

  A cake : pie   **C** truth : lies

  B pages : book   **D** respect : admiration

2. ARIDITY : DESERT : :

  A flatness : plains   **C** courage : danger

  B habitat : woods   **D** flowers : summer

3. STORM : TURBULENT : :

  A rain : wind   **C** sun : chilly

  B breeze : mild   **D** ocean : small

4. REMOTE : NEAR : :

  A close : closer   **C** tall : short

  B small : little   **D** cabin : far

5. VERGE : EDGE : :

  A letter : deliver   **C** under : over

  B peak : top   **D** book : magazine

6. SPIRIT : MOOD : :

  A friend : reserved   **C** center : middle

  B open : jar   **D** scale : weight

7. VERTICAL : UPRIGHT : :

  A reluctant : refuse   **C** warm : balmy

  B decide : decision   **D** obstacle : collapse

8. JOSTLE : SHOVE : :

  A steal : return   **C** music : quiet

  B copy : reproduce   **D** left : right

Circle the letter of the word that is most nearly *opposite* in meaning to the capitalized word.

9. ABRUPTLY

  A lately   **C** suddenly

  B gradually   **D** reasonably

10. AUSTERELY

  A elaborately   **C** fully

  B plainly   **D** hardly

11. CEASED

  A teased   **C** left

  B used   **D** began

12. INTANGIBLE

  A unreal   **C** concrete

  B subtle   **D** pleasant

13. POISED

  A steadied   **C** fascinated

  B imbalanced   **D** bored

14. RIGID

  A false   **C** confused

  B flexible   **D** dry

    Vocabulary in Context G9, SV 9780547625829

Understanding Related Words

The words in the box are closely related to the vocabulary words. See how many of the words you already know. Use the glossary to find definitions of unfamiliar words.

abrupt	arresting	austere	ceaseless	chaotic
remoteness	resilience	rigidity	tangible	turbulence

Match each word in the box with its definition below. Write the matching word on the line.

_____ **1.** going on and on and on

_____ **2.** the ability to spring back into shape or to recover strength or good spirits quickly

_____ **3.** so striking that it makes a person stop and take notice

_____ **4.** violence of motion; uproar

_____ **5.** having actual form or substance; able to be touched

_____ **6.** sudden

_____ **7.** the quality of being distant or secluded

_____ **8.** in a completely confused condition

_____ **9.** the quality of being inflexible

_____ **10.** very plain; without luxury

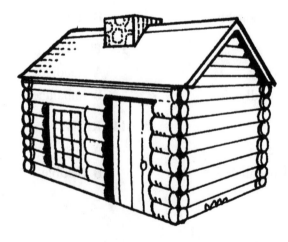

Name _____   Date _____

Answering Questions About Words

Write the letter of the best answer to each question.

_____ 1. If you are on an airplane that is experiencing a great deal of *turbulence*, what would the flight attendant suggest you do?

   A stand up and stretch   **C** eat a sandwich

   B use your oxygen mask   **D** fasten your seat belt

_____ 2. Which of the following would you be most likely to find growing in an *arid* climate?

   A ferns   **B** cactuses   **C** oak trees   **D** vegetables

_____ 3. If the president of the United States suggested that citizens follow an *austerity* program, what would he or she be suggesting they do?

   A vote in every election   **C** buy new cars

   B spend money only on needed things   **D** contribute money to charities

_____ 4. If you entered a *chaotic* daycare center, what would the children there most likely be doing?

   A yelling and running around   **C** rehearsing a play

   B singing a song   **D** taking a test

_____ 5. What would a book on *spiritual* matters be about?

   A mechanics   **B** sports   **C** religion   **D** vocabulary

The Prefix *in-*

The prefix *in-*, which is used in the word *intangible*, has two meanings: (1) in or into, and (2) no, not, or without. The words in the box use *in-*.

| inappropriate | inefficiently | inhabit | inject | inoperative |

Write the word from the box that best completes the meaning of each sentence.

1. Coyotes and armadillos _____ the American Southwest.

2. Until the mechanic gets here to repair the vending machine in the hall, it will be

   _____.

3. Most people think that jeans and a sweatshirt are _____ clothing for a wedding.

4. The researchers had to _____ the rats with medicine.

5. Harold wasted a great deal of time and materials; he did the job very _____.

Understanding Multiple-Meaning Words

Each box in this exercise contains a boldfaced word with its definitions. Read the definitions and then the sentences that use the word. Write the letter of the definition that applies to each sentence.

> **arrest**
> **a.** legal custody (noun)
> **b.** to seize or take into custody by authority of the law (verb)
> **c.** to stop or bring to a halt (verb)

_____ **1.** The officers hope to *arrest* two suspects in the burglary case.

_____ **2.** After placing the suspects under *arrest*, Officer Medrano took them to the police station.

_____ **3.** A lack of water and sunlight can *arrest* the plant's growth.

> **rigid**
> **a.** not bending or flexible; stiff (adjective)
> **b.** severe; strict; not willing to change (adjective)

_____ **4.** As the extra-strength glue dries, it becomes *rigid*.

_____ **5.** The rule against texting in class seems *rigid*, but the reason for it is clear.

_____ **6.** Perhaps it is because Mr. Chung is so *rigid* in his discipline that we were shocked by his laughter.

> **poise**
> **a.** ease and dignity of manner; confidence (noun)
> **b.** to balance; to keep steady; to place in air without support (verb)

_____ **7.** Being a member of the debate team can give a person *poise*.

_____ **8.** The eagle was *poised* on the edge of the cliff, ready to attack.

_____ **9.** Earth is *poised* in space.

Word Skills

Writing

Jack London uses colorful language to describe a favorite place. Write a short description of one of your favorite places. Consider these questions before you write.

• What words or phrases will help your readers picture the place?
• How can you appeal to your readers' senses?
• Is the place remote, or is it somewhere you visit often? Why would someone enjoy being in the place?

Be sure to use some of the vocabulary words from this unit in your description.

_____

_____

_____

_____

_____

_____

_____

_____

_____

_____

_____

_____

Writing

Cave Hunters, Beware!

Read the selection. Think about the meanings of the **boldfaced** words. Then go back to the selection. Underline the words or sentences that give you a clue to the meaning of each **boldfaced** word.

Jennifer Anderson is a spelunker. That word may be strange to you, but for thousands of people like Anderson, it spells fun and excitement. These people practice the hobby of **spelunking** by exploring and studying caves in their leisure time.

Anderson has made spelunking more than a hobby. She has made it her career. Anderson is an experienced spelunker who has explored caves on three continents. She has worked as the editor of a spelunking magazine. She has also served as the head of the National Speleological Society. This is an organization of people who work together to encourage safe spelunking.

Jennifer Anderson knows that spelunkers are usually **adventurers** looking for new challenges. Their **motivation** comes from their desire to explore the unknown. But spelunking is not a pursuit for the careless. Exploring wet, **dank** caves can be very dangerous. A cave has no natural light. Not only could you get lost, but you could also trip over unseen objects. Since most caves are wet, footpaths are usually slippery. Jagged rocks can injure the unlucky spelunker who falls on them. And the walls or ceilings of a cave may not be secure. You could be trapped by falling dirt.

In the book *Cave Exploring*, Anderson alerts new spelunkers to the dangers and advises them to take **precautions** to avoid accidents. For example, she tells spelunkers what **attire** to wear for protection. This includes a helmet with a light, heavy boots, and thick clothing. She also describes how to move safely from place to place. Going down a narrow **passageway**, or tunnel, requires great caution. **Mapping** your route as you go is one way to keep from getting lost. Drawing in landmarks, like unusual rocks, makes the map easy to follow back out of the cave.

Anderson also shares her love of spelunking in her book. She might be compared to a **prospector** looking for gold, except that her search is for a natural wonder, like a room filled with sparkling stalactites.[1] Such discoveries fill Anderson with a joy that is **indescribable**. The moment is so special that there are no words that do it justice!

[1]stalactites: limestone deposits resembling icicles that hang from the ceiling of caves

Context Clues

In each sentence a word or phrase is underlined. Choose a word from the box to replace that word or phrase. Write the word on the line.

adventurers	attire	indescribable	dank	mapping
motivation	passageway	precautions	prospector	spelunking

1. People who enjoy the hobby of exploring caves tend to have a strong sense of adventure.

   _____

2. These individuals who look for excitement and challenges are attracted by the possibility of discovering a cave that no one has explored before.

   _____

3. This possibility is the primary drive that keeps sending them back to explore new caves.

   _____

4. Most cave explorers realize that they must take safety measures that involve planning ahead to avoid accidents.

   _____

5. The first concern is to make sure that they are wearing the proper clothing.

   _____

6. This includes a lighted helmet and warm clothes so that they are prepared for the cold and damp interior of the cave.

   _____

7. They also know to walk very slowly and carefully down a long and narrow tunnel.

   _____

8. Seasoned cave explorers also recall that drawing a representative picture of their route through the cave will help keep them from getting lost.

   _____

9. Most cave explorers make the potentially dangerous trip because they yearn to see natural wonders that are beyond words.

   _____

10. But others play the role of the person looking for gold, hoping to find something of value in the cave that might make them rich.

    _____

Dictionary Skills

Each numbered item has two parts. Answer the first part by writing a word from the box. Answer the second part by circling the correct choice. Use the pronunciation key in a dictionary to help you when necessary.

attire	mapping	precaution	prospector

1. Write the correct spelling of map´ing. _____
   It means   **a.** sleeping.   **b.** drawing a representative picture of.

2. Write the correct spelling of ə tīr´. _____
   It means   **a.** clothes.   **b.** one rubber wheel.

3. Write the correct spelling of pros´pek tər . _____
   It means   **a.** person who looks for gold.   **b.** person who inspects.

4. Write the correct spelling of pri kô´shən . _____
   It means   **a.** afterthought.   **b.** measure taken to avoid problems.

Rewriting Sentences

Rewrite each sentence using one of the vocabulary words in the box.

adventurer	dank	indescribable	motivation	spelunking

1. His need for money was his force that moved him to work.

   _____

2. The air is moist and cold in the cellar.

   _____

3. As a hobby, you can't beat exploring caves for excitement.

   _____

4. My brother is the only true individual who undertakes thrilling and unusual experiences in our family.

   _____

5. The dinner was so delicious that it was beyond words.

   _____

Word Map

Use the words in the box to complete the word map about exploring caves. Add other words that you know to each category. One category will not contain any vocabulary words, but only your own words.

adventurer	attire	motivation	passageways	prospectors

Who Might Explore a Cave

1. _____

2. _____

3. _____

4. _____

5. _____

What Spelunkers See

1. _____

2. _____

3. _____

4. _____

5. _____

EXPLORING CAVES

What Spelunkers Need

1. _____

2. _____

3. _____

4. _____

5. _____

Why Spelunkers Explore

1. _____

2. _____

3. _____

4. _____

5. _____

Vocabulary in Context

Name _____   Date _____

Yes or No?

Read each question. Think about the meaning of the underlined word. Then write *yes* or *no* to answer the question.

1. Could you buy <u>motivation</u> at the hardware store? _____

2. If you want to learn how to find gold, should you ask a <u>prospector</u>? _____

3. Would someone who likes <u>spelunking</u> want to explore a new cave? _____

4. Would it be easy to write about something that is <u>indescribable</u>? _____

5. Is a tropical beach normally <u>dank</u>? _____

6. If you are having trouble with your car, will changing your <u>attire</u> help? _____

7. Is a large room a <u>passageway</u>? _____

Challenge Yourself

1. Name two <u>precautions</u> you might take before going out in a rainstorm.

_____

2. Name two activities that might interest <u>adventurers</u>.

_____

3. Name two times when <u>mapping</u> might be helpful.

_____

Vocabulary in Context

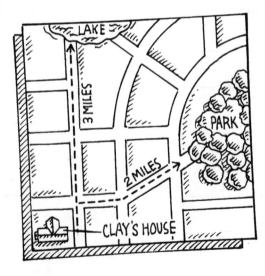

Standardized Test Practice

Circle the letter of the word that best completes the sentence.

TIP

If you are not sure which word completes the sentence, do the best you can. Cross out any answers that are the incorrect part of speech. Then choose the best answer from the choices that are left.

1. Those _____ are always seeking a new thrill.

   A cowards   **B** hobbies   **C** precautions   **D** adventurers

2. If your hobby is _____, you must see a lot of bats.

   A vampires   **B** prospectors   **C** spelunking   **D** cooking

3. By _____ out our route, we will find our way to Florida.

   A swimming   **B** spelunking   **C** forgetting   **D** mapping

4. An explorer's _____ comes from curiosity about the unknown.

   A motivation   **B** packaging   **C** attire   **D** adventurer

5. We wondered where the long _____ would lead.

   A mapping   **B** passageway   **C** attire   **D** flashlight

6. We were glad to get out of that _____ place to a warmer one.

   A motivation   **B** sunny   **C** dank   **D** moisture

7. They took _____ against falling objects by wearing hard hats.

   A prospectors   **B** precautions   **C** attire   **D** adventure

8. The _____ will explore this area for precious minerals.

   A call   **B** spelunking   **C** prospectors   **D** landmarks

9. Wearing formal _____ to a ballgame would be foolish.

   A attire   **B** apparent   **C** dressed   **D** indescribable

10. The cavern is so extraordinary that it is _____.

    A dull   **B** horrible   **C** mapping   **D** indescribable

Understanding Related Words

The words in the box can relate to exploring old caves to learn about ancient peoples. See how many of the words you already know. Use the glossary to find definitions of unfamiliar words.

attribute	authenticate	indelibly	inscribed	perspective
portrayals	preconceptions	prehistoric	scrutiny	visualize

In each sentence a word or phrase is underlined. Choose a word from the box to replace that word or phrase. Write the word on the line. Use the glossary to check the meanings of new words.

1. Modern people hold many opinions formed in advance about ancient people that may not be correct.

   _____

2. One idea is that these people who lived in before-written history-times were savage and crude.

   _____

3. The cave paintings that have been discovered have forced people to change that view.

   _____

4. Once scientists were able to prove the genuineness of these works, people started looking at them closely.

   _____

5. Under this intense close inspection, people recognized the signs of sensitive, artistic talent.

   _____

6. Deep inside dark caves, these artists were able to picture creatures that they drew from memory.

   _____

7. These visual likenesses of everyday animals, such as the horse, bison, and ox, suggested that these animals were important to the ancient people.

   _____

8. Naturally, we cannot know for sure the significance of all of the pictures carved on those stone walls.

   _____

9. However, we can safely credit the choice of those animals to the fact that the ancient people needed them in order to survive.

   _____

10. Fortunately, we have plenty of time to study these paintings, for they are permanently marked on the cave walls.

    _____

Word Skills

Name _____ Date _____

Analogies

An analogy shows the relationship between two pairs of words. Complete each of the following analogies by writing a word from the box on the line.

authenticate	indelibly	inscribed	perspective
prehistoric	scrutiny	visualize	

1. *Now* is to *then* as *modern* is to _____.

2. *Slowly* is to *swiftly* as *temporarily* is to _____.

3. *Definition* is to *meaning* as *viewpoint* is to _____.

4. *Imagine* is to *pretend* as *confirm* is to _____.

5. *Description* is to *described* as *inscription* is to _____.

6. *Voice* is to *speak* as *mind* is to _____.

7. *Peek* is to *glance* as *examination* is to _____.

Word Pairs

Words with similar parts may have related meanings. Study each word pair. Think about how the meanings of the words are alike. Check the meanings in the glossary. Then write a sentence for each word.

1. scrutiny—scrutinize

_____

_____

2. portray—portrayal

_____

_____

3. conceptualize—preconception

_____

_____

4. prehistoric—historic

_____

_____

Vocabulary in Context G9, SV 9780547625829

Word Skills

Word Game

The underlined letters in each sentence below are part of one of the words in the box. Use the underlined letters and the context of the sentence to determine the correct word. Write the word on the line.

attribute	authenticate	indelibly	inscribed	perspective
preconceptions	prehistoric	portrayal	scrutiny	visualize

1. It was just a <u>tiny</u> scar on my forehead, but I always felt that people were <u>giving</u> it a very close look.

   _____

2. His specialty is the study of dinosaurs and other creatures that lived millions of years ago.

   _____

3. On the <u>one</u> hand, she is a very kind person, but on the other hand, she does have a tendency to make judgments about people before she ever meets them.

   _____

4. This artist has created a fabulous painting of a <u>port</u> that looks just like a seacoast town would.

   _____

5. My brother went to a whaling museum and saw pictures that had been carved on whalebones, and he thinks one of the bones was a <u>rib</u>.

   _____

6. <u>Eli</u> spilled black ink on my favorite dress, and now the stain is in the material for good because I cannot seem to wash it out.

   _____

7. I know I should not daydream so much, but sometimes it <u>is</u> more fun to picture in my mind the things I will do when <u>the</u> weekend comes.

   _____

8. He gave a moving <u>tribute</u> to his father, saying that it was his parent who deserved the credit for making him the decent person he is.

   _____

9. Per your request, I have outlined a plan according to the way I <u>see</u> this project developing.

   _____

10. We believe this diamond is real, but <u>then</u> again, we won't know for sure until the jeweler examines it.

   _____

Word Skills

Writing

Jennifer Anderson is enthusiastic about spelunking. She not only enjoys exploring caves, but she has also made a career out of it by writing about her cave explorations.

Write about something that you are enthusiastic about.

• What is something that you are enthusiastic about?
• Is it a sport, a hobby, or something else?
• How could you make a career out of this activity?

Write a paragraph describing the kinds of jobs you might be hired for that relate to this interest. Explain what training or education you would need to pursue this activity as a profession. Use some vocabulary words from this unit in your writing.

_____

_____

_____

_____

_____

_____

_____

_____

_____

_____

_____

Writing

Vocabulary in Context G9, SV 9780547625829

Bill Cosby Gives It Up

Read the selection. Think about the meanings of the **boldfaced** words. Then go back to the selection. Underline the words or sentences that give you a clue to the meaning of each **boldfaced** word.

What does Bill Cosby have in common with Robin Williams and Jim Carrey—besides being funny? In the late 1990s, Cosby's income was around thirty-six million dollars, an amount of money that placed him on *Forbes* magazine's 1997 Top 40 list of the most **prosperous** entertainers. He was there alongside other famous comics like Robin Williams and Jim Carrey.

Jokes aside, Cosby is serious when it comes to money. Cosby has played many roles in television shows, movies, and his stand-up comedy routines, but he equally enjoys the role of giver and helper. As a **benefactor**, Cosby gives out of his own pocket to **disadvantaged** people and other worthy causes. Like other celebrities who make charitable **donations**, such as Oprah Winfrey, Steven Spielberg, and Michael Jordan, he shares his success with others. Frequently, Cosby has performed stand-up routines and given speeches for **benefits** that raise funds for **commendable** causes. He donated twenty million dollars to Spelman College to build a variety of new facilities and pay for teaching positions. Before this, no individual had ever donated such a large amount to an African American college; only three other individual donations to any cause had been larger than his. Cosby and his wife, Camille, also set up a foundation to provide assistance for people with dyslexia, a type of learning disability. The Future Filmmakers Program at New York University was established by Cosby to help encourage and provide opportunities for students in the film industry.

Although his **benevolence** is greatly appreciated, Bill Cosby doesn't donate for **recognition** or fame; his acts of charity come from his heart and from his belief that the road to success starts with one important word—*education*. This belief could seem kind of funny coming from somebody who was better at cracking up his friends in class than cracking open a book. However, Cosby was determined to achieve his goals, despite his **resistance** to schoolwork. Because he was a natural comedian but not a natural student, his road to success was not straight and immediate. At one point, he even dropped out of high school. Nicknamed Shorty because he was tall as a kid, Shorty did not come up short; he realized that he would never really succeed in a personal way if he didn't have some solid ground under him, and that ground was education. He showed great **perseverance** by continuing to work on his degrees even as he achieved success working in the entertainment industry. He became so focused on his goal that he eventually earned a Ph.D. in education—no joke. Although it may seem that Cosby's dream was to be in the spotlight, his personal dream was to finish college. You could say that education is no laughing matter to Bill Cosby, and donating his income to educational causes shows how serious he is.

Name _____ Date _____

Context Clues

Use context clues from the selection to match the vocabulary word from the box with its definition below. Write the word on the line. Use the glossary for help if you need to.

| benefactor | benefits | benevolence | commendable | disadvantaged |
| donations | recognition | resistance | perseverance | prosperous |

1. _____: wealthy and successful

2. _____: credit or appreciation

3. _____: person who makes a gift or donation

4. _____: worthy of praise

5. _____: events intended to make money for a cause

6. _____: gifts or contributions

7. _____: steady action or belief, usually over a long period of time

8. _____: lacking basic resources, such as food and housing

9. _____: generosity and helpfulness, often toward people who are suffering

10. _____: opposition to something or somebody

Vocabulary in Context G9, SV 9780547625829

Name _____ Date _____

Word Game

The underlined letters in each sentence below can be used in one of the words in the box. Use the underlined letters and the context of the sentence to determine the correct word. Write the word on the line.

benefactor	benefits	benevolence	commendable	disadvantaged
donations	recognition	resistance	perseverance	prosperous

Vocabulary in Context

1. The celebrity told his agent to fit all the charity events into his busy calendar. _____

2. People who do not have access to food and shelter often age faster than people with more resources. _____

3. Ben is such a kindhearted person that he often spends his spare time helping his friends. _____

4. The bike club gave my neighbor an award for her years of effort campaigning for new bike lanes, which were finally approved by the city council last week. _____

5. Don gives generously to many good causes. _____

6. After all our hard work, it felt good when the principal praised us in her speech. _____

7. The actress may have plenty of money, but the fact remains that she is incredibly generous to other artists in her field. _____

8. Roberto and Martha really don't want to get a tan this afternoon because they are aware of the damage that ultraviolet rays can do to the skin. _____

9. I wasn't sure if I'd be able to express how worthy this cause truly is. _____

10. The former athlete is certainly making a good living; she charges $10,000 per speech, and she often gives several speeches a month. _____

Understanding Multiple-Meaning Words

Each box contains a boldfaced word with its definitions. Read the definitions and then the sentences that use the word. Write the letter of the definition that applies to each sentence.

> **benefit**
> **a.** to give or receive help or advantage (verb)
> **b.** event intended to make money for a cause (noun)
> **c.** something that has a good effect or promotes well-being (noun)
> **d.** payment made by an employer or an insurance company (noun)

_____ **1.** The *benefit* raised ten thousand dollars for cancer research.

_____ **2.** He *benefits* from regular exercise and a healthful diet.

_____ **3.** My company offers medical *benefits* after ninety days of employment.

_____ **4.** One *benefit* of going to bed early is an ability to concentrate in the morning.

> **recognition**
> **a.** a knowledge or feeling of having encountered someone before (noun)
> **b.** credit or appreciation (noun)

_____ **5.** Li and Alonzo deserve *recognition* for all their hard work on the art project.

_____ **6.** The man gave me a look of *recognition*, but it wasn't until we started talking that I realized he was my former soccer coach.

> **commend**
> **a.** to praise someone or something (verb)
> **b.** to entrust somebody or yourself to somebody else's safekeeping (verb)

_____ **7.** The prospector *commended* his children to the local schoolteacher and promised to return with enough gold to pay her generously.

_____ **8.** I *commended* my friends for a job well done after they organized a great surprise birthday party.

True-False

Decide whether each statement is true (T) or false (F). Write *T* or *F* for each statement.

_____   **1.** If you are feeling *resistance* to going to school, you would get up early to be sure to catch the bus on time.

_____   **2.** The main goal of a *benefit* is to get dressed up and have fun.

_____   **3.** If you do something for the *recognition*, you would make sure everyone knew you were doing it.

_____   **4.** Someone who is *prosperous* would probably beg for money.

_____   **5.** Gifts made to charities are considered *donations*.

_____   **6.** If you complete a difficult project after many months, people would praise your *perseverance*.

_____   **7.** *Disadvantaged* people generally live in mansions.

_____   **8.** A *benefactor* might give a new artist money and a place to work.

Challenge Yourself

1. Name two examples of benevolence.

_____

2. Name two commendable things you have done.

_____

3. Name two signs that someone is prosperous.

_____

Standardized Test Practice

Circle the letter of the word that is a synonym of the capitalized word.

TIP

Remember that synonyms have similar meanings. To help you decide the correct answer, cross out any answer choices that do not have similar meanings.

1. BENEVOLENCE
   A violence   **B** kindness   **C** despair   **D** silence

2. COMMENDABLE
   A praiseworthy   **B** wealthy   **C** fixable   **D** loving

3. DISADVANTAGED
   A confused   **B** lucky   **C** poor   **D** disorganized

4. DONATIONS
   A contacts   **B** contributions   **C** losses   **D** sales

5. PROSPEROUS
   A old   **B** rich   **C** tired   **D** funny

6. RECOGNITION
   A sorrow   **B** reunion   **C** intelligence   **D** credit

7. RESISTANCE
   A excitement   **B** health   **C** spending   **D** opposition

Circle the letter of the word or words that best complete the sentence.

8. A *benefactor* is someone who
   A is friendly to everyone.   **C** gives money or resources.
   B counts money for a living.   **D** works hard at a difficult job.

9. People organize *benefits* mainly to
   A have a night out on the town.   **C** introduce new comics.
   B advertise their new product.   **D** make money for a cause.

10. Someone might tell you that you showed *perseverance* if you
    A ate too much.   **C** slept a lot.
    B worked hard.   **D** gave up.

Understanding Related Words

The words in the box are used in sentences about a famous actor. See how many of the words you already know. Use the glossary to find definitions of unfamiliar words.

acceptance	confined	conventional	disadvantage	ethnic
evoke	exposure	expressive	instill	involvement

Use context clues and your knowledge of word parts to determine which word from the box goes on each line. Then reread the paragraphs to be sure they make sense. Use the glossary if necessary.

Hector Elizondo grew up in a very diverse neighborhood in New York City. At first Elizondo was worried he would be typecast in only Hispanic roles. He did not want his career to be _____ in that way. His _____ to, or contact with, many different _____ groups helped to _____ in him the ability to portray characters of many different cultures and nationalities. Elizondo has never found his background to be a _____, or obstacle. As a result, he has played many _____ roles, as well as nontraditional ones. Elizondo's _____ face and voice convince his audiences that he really is whatever character he plays. It seems easy for him to _____ responses of laughter, tears, or sympathy.

Elizondo's _____ in popular television shows has made him well known to the public. He is happy that he has gained _____ by the entertainment industry and has earned national recognition.

Antonyms

Remember that antonyms are words with opposite meanings. Match the words in the box with their antonyms listed below. Write each word on the line.

acceptance	confined	conventional	disadvantage
evoke	expressive	instill	

1. emotionless _____

2. benefit _____

3. free _____

4. rejection _____

5. unusual _____

6. suppress _____

7. erode _____

Name Game

1. Name two ways of gaining the <u>acceptance</u> of coworkers.

_____

2. Name two <u>conventional</u> ways of getting to work.

_____

3. Name two ways of achieving <u>involvement</u> in the life of your community.

_____

4. Name two ways a baseball team can <u>evoke</u> cheers from a crowd.

_____

Word Skills

Word Origins

Knowing the origin of a word can help you understand its meaning. Read each word origin. Then write each word from the box next to its origin.

acceptance	confined	ethnic
evoke	exposure	instill

1. from the Latin *accipere*, to receive _____

2. from the Latin *exposer*, to expose _____

3. from the Latin *evocare*, to call forth _____

4. from the Latin *confin*, boundary _____

5. from the Latin *instillare*, to drip in _____

6. from the Greek *ethnikos*, of a national group _____

Writing Sentences

Use each word in the box to write an original sentence.

acceptance	disadvantage	conventional
expressive	exposure	involvement

1. _____

2. _____

3. _____

4. _____

5. _____

6. _____

Word Skills

Writing

Bill Cosby gives money and time to causes he feels are commendable. Think of a cause that is important to you. Write a paragraph explaining why you would contribute time and money to this cause. Consider these questions before you write.

- Whom or what would you be helping?
- How would your time and money help the cause?

Be sure to use some of the vocabulary words from this unit in your writing.

_____

_____

_____

_____

_____

_____

_____

_____

_____

_____

_____

_____

Writing

Vocabulary in Context G9, SV 9780547625829

Fighting Germs

Read the selection. Think about the meanings of the **boldfaced** words. Then go back to the selection. Underline the words or sentences that give you a clue to the meaning of each **boldfaced** word.

Until the twentieth century, **surgical** patients often died of a bacterial infection. As doctors learned more about disease, it became clear that simple cleanliness could help prevent the spread of some **infectious** diseases. Today, hospitals and clinics use a variety of technologies to prevent the spread of some diseases. For example, ultraviolet **radiation**, boiling water, and chemicals are used in health facilities to kill **pathogens**, or germs.

During the mid-1800s, Louis Pasteur, a French scientist, discovered that tiny germs, or **microorganisms**, cause wine to spoil. The uninvited microorganisms were bacteria. Pasteur **contrived** a method of using heat to kill most of the bacteria in the wine. This method is called pasteurization, and it is still used today.

In the late 1700s, no one knew what a pathogen was. It was during this time that Edward Jenner, a physician, studied a disease called smallpox. He observed that people who had been infected with cowpox seemed to have protection against smallpox. This protection, or resistance to a disease, is called **immunity**. Jenner's work led to the first modern vaccine. A **vaccine** is a substance that helps your body develop immunity to a disease.

Today, vaccines are used all over the world to prevent many serious diseases. Modern vaccines contain pathogens that are killed or specially treated so that they can't make you very sick. The vaccine is enough like the pathogen to allow your body to develop a defense against the disease.

Bacterial infections can be **perilous** to your health. Fortunately, doctors can usually treat these kinds of infections with antibiotics. An **antibiotic** is a substance that can kill bacteria or slow the growth of bacteria. Antibiotics may also be used to treat infections caused by other microorganisms, like fungi. If you take an antibiotic when you are sick, it is important that you take it according to your doctor's instructions, to ensure that all the pathogens are killed.

Context Clues

Use context clues from the selection to help you complete the sentences below with the correct vocabulary word. Write the word on the line. Use the glossary for help if you need to.

antibiotic	contrived	immunity	infectious	microorganisms
pathogens	perilous	radiation	surgical	vaccine

1. The child received a _____ for chickenpox so that she would not get the disease.

2. One way that hospitals prevent the spread of diseases is through ultraviolet

   _____.

3. The doctors _____ a brilliant treatment plan for my grandmother, and she felt better in a couple of months.

4. My doctor gave me a(n) _____ to clear up my bacterial infection.

5. Selina was not worried about contracting the disease because the vaccine had given her

   _____.

6. It can be _____ to your health to let a bacterial infection go untreated.

7. They examined the _____ under a microscope to see exactly what they were.

8. It is important to wash your hands often to prevent the spread of _____ diseases.

9. If a condition does not respond to medicine, doctors may consider _____ options; however, operations are not always possible.

10. Bacteria and viruses are both _____ because they cause diseases.

Name _____ Date _____

Rewriting Sentences

Rewrite each sentence using one of the vocabulary words in the box.

antibiotic	contrived	pathogens	radiation	vaccine

1. Energy emitted from ultraviolet rays is used to prevent illnesses at hospitals.

   _____

2. He came up with a clever method for cleaning hospital rooms.

   _____

3. To prevent the spread of smallpox, doctors gave their patients a substance that helps the body develop immunity to a disease.

   _____

4. After getting a sinus infection, William got a prescription for a substance that would kill the bacteria.

   _____

5. The laboratory contained samples of many different types of things that can cause diseases.

   _____

True-False

Decide whether each statement is true (T) or false (F). Write *T* or *F* for each statement.

_____ 1. If a patient has *immunity* to a disease, he or she will likely get it.

_____ 2. An *infectious* disease can be passed from one person to another.

_____ 3. *Microorganisms* are about the size of a golf ball.

_____ 4. It is likely that your family and teachers would ask you to try a *perilous* activity.

_____ 5. A *surgical* doctor performs operations.

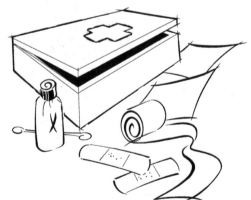

Vocabulary in Context G9, SV 9780547625829

Understanding Multiple-Meaning Words

Each box contains a boldfaced word with its definitions. Read the definitions and then the sentences that use the word. Write the letter of the definition that applies to each sentence.

> **contrived**
> **a.** made or invented something (verb)
> **b.** brought about with difficulty; managed (verb)
> **c.** having a false appearance or quality (adjective)

_____ **1.** She *contrived* a brilliant plan to improve the lunch menu.

_____ **2.** Since we knew the actors didn't like each other, we all thought the love story in the movie seemed *contrived*.

_____ **3.** The politician began far behind in the poll numbers, but she *contrived* to win the support of some of her opponent's most loyal followers.

> **immunity**
> **a.** freedom from something unpleasant (noun)
> **b.** resistance to a particular disease (noun)

_____ **4.** Being exposed to some pathogens can lead to future *immunity*.

_____ **5.** He gained *immunity* from prosecution in exchange for information about his company's illegal activities.

> **infectious**
> **a.** capable of being easily spread (adjective)
> **b.** capable of causing an infection (adjective)

_____ **6.** My friend Jorge has the most *infectious* laughter; when he starts laughing, the whole room ends up in fits of giggles.

_____ **7.** We were told these were *infectious* viruses.

Name _____ Date _____

Word Groups

As you read each pair of words, think about how they are alike. Write the word from the box that best completes each group.

contrived	immunity	infectious	microorganisms	perilous

1. resistance, protection, _____

2. viruses, bacteria, _____

3. planned, made, _____

4. catching, transferable, _____

5. dangerous, risky, _____

Challenge Yourself

1. Name two instances when you might need a vaccine.

_____

2. Name two types of jobs you might do in the surgical unit of a hospital.

_____

3. Name something you could use to look at a microorganism.

_____

Vocabulary in Context

Standardized Test Practice

Circle the letter of the word or words that best complete the sentence.

 TIP

Always read all the answer choices. Many choices may make sense, but only one answer choice has the same meaning as the italicized word.

1. You would most likely take an *antibiotic* if you had a

   A bacterial infection.

   B sprained ankle.

   C fear of surgery.

   D bad night's sleep.

2. The word *contrived* means

   A confused.

   B prescribed.

   C planned.

   D examined.

3. If a person had *immunity* to a disease, he or she would most likely

   A get it.

   B fight it off.

   C give it to someone else.

   D diagnose it.

4. Another word for *infectious* is

   A unclean.

   B deadly.

   C disease.

   D transferable.

5. *Microorganisms* are all very

   A small.

   B deadly.

   C rare.

   D cold.

6. *Pathogens* are

   A doctors that study deadly diseases.

   B hospital equipment that kills diseases.

   C disease-causing agents.

   D medications that cure illnesses.

7. A condition that can be *perilous* to your health is

   A effective.

   B dangerous.

   C expensive.

   D harmless.

8. *Radiation* is a type of

   A medication.

   B hospital.

   C liquid.

   D energy.

9. A *surgical* unit in a hospital is where doctors

   A send patients for physical therapy.

   B treat only children.

   C perform operations.

   D see new patients with colds.

10. If a person received a *vaccine* for smallpox, his or her chances of getting smallpox would most likely

    A go up significantly.

    B go up slightly.

    C stay the same.

    D go down.

Understanding Related Words

The words in the box can be related to the theme of medicine. See how many of the words you already know. Use the glossary to find definitions of unfamiliar words.

contrast	devise	distinctly	earphones	electrical
electron	illusion	miniature	portable	visual

Read each sentence. Look for clues to help you complete the sentence with a word from the box. Write the word on the line.

1. The practice of medicine is _____ different from the way it was in the past.

2. Doctors can use movable, or _____, cameras to send information about their patients to other doctors.

3. Doctors can monitor how well a heart is working by reading charts that show its

   _____ activity.

4. There is a great _____ between the medical tools used today and those used in the past.

5. Cameras provide doctors with _____ messages so that they can see possible health problems.

6. Movable cameras have _____ beams that photograph a patient.

7. Today's healthcare workers have been able to _____ ways to help wheelchair users get around in new places.

8. Students in wheelchairs can wear special helmets with _____ that send sounds to the students.

9. These helmets also allow students to see small floor plans on _____ screens built into the headsets.

10. The images give students the _____ that they are moving about in a real-life situation, preparing them for what they may really experience!

Antonyms

Remember that antonyms are words with opposite meanings. Match the words in the box with their antonyms listed below. Write each word on the line.

distinctly	miniature	portable

1. vaguely _____

2. immovable _____

3. huge _____

Dictionary Skills

Each item below has two parts. Answer the first part by writing a word from the box. Answer the second part by circling the correct choice. Use the pronunciation key in a dictionary to help you when necessary.

contrast	devise	distinctly	electrical	electron	illusion

1. Write the correct spelling of di vīz´. _____
   It means   **a.** invent.   **b.** destroy.

2. Write the correct spelling of i lek´tron. _____
   It means   **a.** a kind of car.   **b.** a kind of beam.

3. Write the correct spelling of kon´trast. _____
   It means   **a.** a difference.   **b.** a similarity.

4. Write the correct spelling of i lü´zhen. _____
   It means   **a.** a trick.   **b.** a dance.

5. Write the correct spelling of di stingkt´lē. _____
   It means   **a.** noisily.   **b.** definitely.

6. Write the correct spelling of i lek´tri kəl. _____
   It means   **a.** related to a city.   **b.** related to electricity.

Word Skills

Completing Sentences

Choose the word that best completes the sentence. Write the letter of the correct word on the line.

_____ **1.** The word *distinctly* means

A happily.   B definitely.   C hardly.   D closely.

_____ **2.** *Electron* beams on television carry

A cameras.   B radios.   C pictures.   D earphones.

_____ **3.** A *contrast* is a kind of

A device.   B contract.   C similarity.   D difference.

_____ **4.** Something *portable* is an item you can

A break.   B carry.   C wash.   D hear.

_____ **5.** Something you *devise* is something you

A divide.   B purchase.   C create.   D borrow.

_____ **6.** An *illusion* is a kind of

A trick.   B tool.   C reality.   D paint.

_____ **7.** *Earphones* are used for

A viewing.   B reading.   C listening.   D humming.

_____ **8.** A *visual* display can be

A hidden.   B chosen.   C broken.   D seen.

_____ **9.** Something *miniature* is

A tiny.   B lazy.   C enormous.   D lovely.

_____ **10.** Something *electrical* uses

A batteries.   B electricity.   C film.   D television.

Writing

You have read about advances in medicine. Write a paragraph explaining what you know about staying healthy after reading this unit and from other sources.

- What are pathogens?
- How can you build your immunity?
- When should you take an antibiotic?
- What else do you know about ways to stay healthy?

Be sure to use some of the vocabulary words from this unit in your writing.

_____

_____

_____

_____

_____

_____

_____

_____

_____

_____

_____

Writing

The Railroad Excursion

Read the selection. Think about the meanings of the **boldfaced** words. Then go back to the selection. Underline the words or sentences that give you a clue to the meaning of each **boldfaced** word.

In 1881, one of the most adventurous ways to travel was by railroad. In that year Ben Travis, age fifteen, took his first railroad **excursion**. Ben traveled with his father from Omaha, Nebraska, to Sacramento, California. They rode the Pacific Express, covering a distance of almost 2,000 miles!

The Express had been in service for a dozen years. Its **operation** was made possible on that famous date, May 15, 1869, when the eastern and western rail lines were linked up at Promontory, Utah. When the railroad was opened, travel from the Midwest to California was **transformed**. Instead of taking six months by wagon train, it became possible for passengers to arrive at their **destination** in less than a week. The train route also affected the number of people making the trip. In the first full year that the line operated, almost 150,000 people rode the train to California. In 1881, nearly a million people made the same trip!

Ben's school semester had just ended, and his father was taking him to spend part of his summer with his grandparents, who lived in San Francisco. When the day came to start their trip, Ben eagerly boarded the train. He made sure he was one of the first passengers to board so he would have a window seat. He didn't want to miss any of the **fascinating** sights along the way.

As they crossed the Great Plains, Ben watched intently for herds of buffalo. Although he sometimes saw a few small herds off in the distance, he never saw the enormous numbers that he had read about in stories. Since the train did not have any dining facilities, it stopped at stations along the way for meals. After several of these stops, Ben and his father were grateful that the trip would last only a few days. The meals, whether breakfast, lunch, or supper, were **monotonous**: beefsteak, fried potatoes, and fried eggs. Occasionally, there might be an alternative dish, such as the breakfast that some passengers thought was chicken stew but was actually prairie dog.

After crossing the plains, the train began climbing into the higher **elevations** of the Rocky Mountains. Ben had never seen anything like these mountains. He could look at their endless variety of features and imagine them to be shaped like a **profile**, a staircase, or even a castle. There were also any number of small streams, formed from melting snow, flowing down the mountainsides and **cascading** into waterfalls as they flowed into the larger streams of the valleys.

Ben enjoyed traveling through the mountains more than any other part of the trip, but soon they were in California, nearing the end of the line. After a few more hours they finally arrived at their last stop, Sacramento. Ben found his grandparents waiting on the station **platform**.

Context Clues

Use context clues from the selection to help you match the definition with the correct word from the box. Write the word on the line. Use the glossary for help if you need to.

| cascading | destination | elevations | excursion | fascinating |
| monotonous | operation | platform | profiles | transformed |

1. _____: flowing quickly and in large amounts

2. _____: inspiring a lot of interest

3. _____: the place where someone is going

4. _____: changed

5. _____: heights

6. _____: the state of being functional or in effect

7. _____: the outlines of people's faces, seen from the side

8. _____: boring because of being repetitive and unvaried

9. _____: a raised structure at a rail station where passengers can board and others can wait for passengers

10. _____: a usually short trip

Word Game

The underlined letters in each sentence below can be used in one of the words in the box. Use the underlined letters and the context of the sentence to determine the correct word. Write the word on the line.

cascading	destination	elevations	excursions	fascinating
monotonous	operation	platform	profiles	transformed

1. Every sight we see on our journey <u>is</u> as interesting and delightful as the last.

   _____

2. <u>On</u> the tall peaks, mountain climbers felt they could see the entire world.

   _____

3. The children <u>formed</u> a semicircle to watch a movie showing the process of a caterpillar changing into a butterfly.

   _____

4. Teresa finally arrived at the camp after traveling for days across this vast <u>nation</u>.

   _____

5. We all worked sixty hours <u>per</u> week to get the factory ready to become functional.

   _____

6. After watching the same movie four times, Joe told his sister he would <u>not</u> be joining her for a fifth showing.

   _____

7. The photographer captured the outlines of the women's faces as they gazed out to the ocean from the <u>pier</u>.

   _____

8. Robert and his <u>ex</u> used to take many weekend trips to new locations.

   _____

9. It is simply good <u>form</u> to wait patiently for train passengers in the designated <u>areas</u>.

   _____

10. My favorite <u>ad</u> shows water gushing down a waterfall in a beautiful setting.

   _____

100

Understanding Multiple-Meaning Words

Each box contains a boldfaced word with its definitions. Read the definitions and then the sentences that use the word. Write the letter of the definition that applies to each sentence.

---

operation

a. the state of being functional or in effect (noun)

b. a medical procedure that involves surgery (noun)

c. an organized action, especially one carried out by the police or military (noun)

d. a mathematical process; for example, subtraction, addition, or multiplication (noun)

e. an illegal or dishonest business (noun)

_____ **1.** The police suspected that the Johnsons were running a shady *operation*.

_____ **2.** Jai had an *operation* to remove her tonsils.

_____ **3.** After weeks of preparation, the plant is finally in *operation*.

_____ **4.** The rescue *operation* lasted through the night, and the missing child was found safely in the early morning hours.

_____ **5.** Our math teacher showed us how to perform that *operation* on our own without a calculator.

---

platform

a. a raised structure at a rail station where passengers can board and others can wait for passengers (noun)

b. a raised level of flooring for performers or speakers (noun)

c. the policies of a political party seeking election (noun)

d. a computer operating system (noun)

e. a position of authority or fame that provides a good opportunity for doing something (noun)

_____ **6.** Being a celebrity gave Callie the *platform* to spread the word about the need for clean drinking water.

_____ **7.** I asked if the new software was compatible with my computer's *platform*.

_____ **8.** The senator ran for reelection on a *platform* of financial responsibility.

_____ **9.** Lori and Kristi waited on the *platform* for Amy's train.

_____ **10.** The speaker stood on the *platform* so that her audience could see her.

Vocabulary in Context

> **profile**
> **a.** the outline of someone's face, seen from the side (noun)
> **b.** a short account of someone's life or activities (noun)
> **c.** a level of how noticeable someone or something is (noun)
> **d.** to write or present a short account of someone's life or activities (verb)

_____ **11.** The lawyer worked on a high *profile* case.

_____ **12.** With his long nose and broad chin, he had a striking *profile*.

_____ **13.** The journalist will *profile* the senator on this week's program.

_____ **14.** I wrote a *profile* of my art teacher for the school newspaper.

> **excursion**
> **a.** a usually short trip (noun)
> **b.** a group of people on a short trip together (noun)
> **c.** a temporary change of direction or topic (noun)

_____ **15.** The *excursion* traveled to Montreal for the long weekend.

_____ **16.** The family took an *excursion* to Boston for the weekend.

_____ **17.** Although Mr. Binoche usually stuck to his teaching plan, he sometimes took *excursions* into unrelated personal stories.

> **cascading**
> **a.** flowing quickly and in large amounts (adjective)
> **b.** hanging or lying in a flowing mass (verb)
> **c.** arranging the windows on a computer screen so they overlap (verb)

_____ **18.** Her long black hair was *cascading* down her back.

_____ **19.** The *cascading* waterfall was a sight to see.

_____ **20.** I was *cascading* the windows on my screen so I could see what programs I had open.

Standardized Test Practice

Circle the letter of the word that is a synonym of the capitalized word.

> **TIP**
>
> Be sure to read all the answers before choosing the correct one.

1. CASCADING

   A using   **B** flowing   **C** typing   **D** washing

2. ELEVATIONS

   A volumes   **B** stairs   **C** heights   **D** celebrations

3. EXCURSION

   A test   **B** journey   **C** manager   **D** train

4. FASCINATING

   A snobby   **B** humorous   **C** excited   **D** interesting

5. MONOTONOUS

   A lonely   **B** dull   **C** tired   **D** clever

6. TRANSFORMED

   A wrote   **B** moved   **C** held   **D** changed

Circle the letter of the word or words that best complete the sentence.

7. A *destination* is a

   A journey's end.   **B** lasting impression.   **C** new country.   **D** good fortune.

8. If a business is in *operation*, it is

   A broke.   **B** wealthy.   **C** open.   **D** closed.

9. On a railroad *platform*, you could

   A look out the window at the scenery.   **C** hail a taxicab.

   B travel to another city.   **D** wait for a passenger.

10. If you notice *profiles*, you are interested in people's

    A hands.   **B** faces.   **C** shoes.   **D** necklaces.

Understanding Related Words

The words in the box can be related to having adventures. They are used here in sentences about mountain climbing. See how many of the words you already know. Use the glossary to find definitions of unfamiliar words.

abyss	bracing	committed	formidable	impassable
instinctively	merged	precipice	surmount	zenith

Use context clues to replace the underlined word or phrase with a word from the box. Write the word on the line. Use the glossary if necessary.

1. Climbing a mountain is a <u>forbidding</u> task.   _____

2. A climber must be very <u>dedicated to completing the task</u> to try such a dangerous feat.   _____

3. There are so many problems and hardships to <u>overcome</u> during a mountain climb.   _____

4. Climbers are challenged by one <u>very steep cliff</u> after another.   _____

5. There is the constant danger of falling into an <u>extremely deep crack in the earth</u>.   _____

6. A trail may suddenly become <u>not fit for traveling over</u> because of falling rocks or snow and ice.   _____

7. Blowing snow can play tricks with a climber's vision so that separate objects seem <u>blended together</u>.   _____

8. Fortunately, a good climber learns to make decisions <u>using knowledge he or she is born with</u>.   _____

9. For example, a climber may know just when <u>giving support to</u> his or her arms, legs, or back will prevent a fall.   _____

10. And an experienced climber knows how to read the sky and to predict the number of hours from the time the sun reaches its <u>point directly overhead</u> to the hour when it sets.   _____

www.harcourtschoolsupply.com
104
Unit 10
Vocabulary in Context G9, SV 9780547625829

Word Skills

Analogies

An analogy shows the relationship between pairs of words. Use the words in the box to complete the following analogies.

abyss	committed	formidable	merged	precipice	surmount

1. *Controlled* is to *regulated* as _____ is to *dedicated*.

2. *Rigid* is to *flexible* as _____ is to *easy*.

3. *Peak* is to *height* as _____ is to *depth*.

4. *Wave* is to *ocean* as _____ is to *mountain*.

5. *Surrender* is to *yield* as _____ is to *overcome*.

6. *Bloomed* is to *wilted* as _____ is to *separated*.

Word Descriptions

Read each word description. Then write the word from the box that best fits each description. Refer to the glossary if you need help.

bracing	impassable	instinctively	surmount	zenith

1. You might use this word to describe what purpose a column serves for a building. _____

2. This word describes what roads are like during a blizzard or a flood. _____

3. This word tells what determined people try to do when they meet an obstacle. _____

4. You can use this word to describe the place where the sun usually is at noon. _____

5. To explain how birds know when it is time to migrate south for the winter, you would use this word. _____

Word Skills

Cloze Sentences

Choose the word that best completes the sentence. Write the letter of the correct word on the line.

_____ 1. When the kitten caught sight of the dog, she _____ hissed and arched her back.
   A illegally   B calm   C formidable   D instinctively

_____ 2. Marcos was the president of the club, so he was _____ to attending all meetings.
   A committed   B merged   C voted   D credited

_____ 3. The wrestler was huge and looked like a _____ opponent.
   A bracing   B helpless   C formidable   D merged

_____ 4. To enter the highway, the car _____ into the right lane.
   A merged   B crashed   C encircled   D committed

_____ 5. He didn't fall because he was _____ himself against the wall.
   A bracing   B painting   C attracting   D surmounting

_____ 6. The mountain goat was trapped on a steep _____ and could not get down.
   A building   B boundary   C abyss   D precipice

_____ 7. The landslide blocked the cave entrance, making it _____ to us.
   A open   B committed   C impassable   D broken

_____ 8. As her pick fell down into the icy _____, the climber sighed with frustration.
   A acre   B machinery   C precipice   D abyss

_____ 9. At the _____ of its power, Rome ruled all of Europe.
   A coolest   B side   C zenith   D precipice

_____ 10. By taking swimming lessons, Jill hopes to _____ her fear of the water.
   A surmount   B continue   C brace   D explain

Word Skills

Name _____ Date _____

Writing

You have learned vocabulary words related to two very different types of adventures, riding in a train for the first time and mountain climbing. Think of other adventures you have read about.

Describe an adventure you have experienced.

- What did you do? What made it an adventure?
- What obstacles, if any, did you have to surmount?
- How did you feel during the adventure?

Be sure to use some of the vocabulary words from this unit in your writing.

_____

_____

_____

_____

_____

_____

_____

_____

_____

_____

Writing

Glossary

A

abrupt	*adjective*	sudden (page 64)
abruptly	*adverb*	unexpectedly (page 58)
abyss	*noun*	a very deep space (page 104)
accelerated	*verb*	caused to go faster (page 18)
acceptance	*noun*	approval (page 84)
accessible	*adjective*	easily obtained (page 18)
adjacent	*adjective*	next to; near (page 28)
adornments	*noun*	decorations (page 48)
adventurers	*noun*	people who do unusual, exciting things (page 68)
airtight	*adjective*	not allowing air to get in or out (page 34)
altimeter	*noun*	a device that measures altitude, or height above the ground (page 18)
amazingly	*adverb*	in an astonishing or surprising way (page 24)
antibiotic	*noun*	a substance that can kill or slow the growth of bacteria (page 88)
architecture	*noun*	the planning and designing of buildings (page 54)
arid	*adjective*	dry (page 65)
aridity	*noun*	the condition of being dry and barren (page 58)
arrested	*verb*	stopped or checked the motion, course, or spread of (page 58)
arresting	*adjective*	so striking that it makes a person stop and take notice (page 64)
artistry	*noun*	skillful work by artists (page 48)
attire	*noun*	clothing (page 68)
attribute	*verb*	to name as a cause or source (page 74)
austere	*adjective*	very plain; without luxury (page 64)
austerely	*adverb*	harshly; severely; plainly (page 58)
austerity	*noun*	plainness (page 65)
authenticate	*verb*	to prove; to show to be true (page 74)
authorization	*noun*	the giving of power or command (page 55)
authorized	*verb*	gave power to (page 54)

B

bedrock	*noun*	solid rock just beneath Earth's surface (page 34)
belated	*adjective*	delayed; overdue (page 39)
belligerent	*adjective*	warlike; quarrelsome; inclined to show hostility or aggression (page 38)
benefactor	*noun*	person who makes a gift or donation (page 78)
benefits	*noun*	events intended to make money for a cause (page 78)
benevolence	*noun*	an act of kindness; a generous gift (page 78)
bounteous	*adjective*	provided in abundance; plentiful (page 38)
bracing	*noun*	the act of holding something in place (page 104)

burrow	*noun*	a hole or tunnel dug by an animal (page 8)

C

cascading	*verb*	flowing quickly and in large amounts (pages 98, 102)
cascading	*adjective*	hanging or lying in a flowing mass; arranging the windows on a computer screen so they overlap (page 102)
casualties	*noun*	deaths or serious injuries (page 34)
ceased	*verb*	stopped (page 58)
ceaseless	*adjective*	going on and on and on (page 64)
chaos	*noun*	disorder (page 58)
chaotic	*adjective*	in a completely confused condition (page 64)
citadel	*noun*	fortress; safe place (pages 48, 50)
clarity	*noun*	sharpness of focus; clearness (page 24)
closeness	*noun*	nearness in space or in feeling (page 24)
colleagues	*noun*	fellow workers (page 8)
colonize	*verb*	to settle in a new country; to establish a colony or community of people (page 48)
commemorate	*verb*	to honor the memory of (page 48)
commendable	*adjective*	worthy of praise (page 78)
committed	*adjective*	dedicated to a course of action (page 104)
completion	*noun*	condition of being finished (page 54)
components	*noun*	ingredients (page 9)
comprises	*verb*	consists of; includes (page 34)
conceptualize	*verb*	to form an idea of (page 75)
conducted	*verb*	led to; directed the course of (page 18)
confined	*verb*	limited; held back (page 84)
contemptuous	*adjective*	scornful (page 38)
contraptions	*noun*	devices or machines (page 24)
contrast	*noun*	a great difference between things (page 94)
contrived	*adjective*	having a false appearance or quality (page 91)
contrived	*verb*	made or invented something; brought about with difficulty; managed (page 88)
controversy	*noun*	a discussion in which people oppose each other (page 45)
conventional	*adjective*	usual, traditional (page 84)
convert	*verb*	to change from one form or belief to another; to exchange for something of equal value (page 45)
correspondence	*noun*	written messages (page 24)
creation	*noun*	the act of making something new; something new (page 55)
creativity	*noun*	imagination; the ability to invent or design (page 54)
cumbersome	*adjective*	awkward to carry (page 48)

Vocabulary in Context G9, SV 9780547625829

D

dank	*adjective*	unpleasantly cold and wet (page 68)
demonstrated	*verb*	showed; proved (page 28)
demonstrative	*adjective*	openly showing one's feelings (page 30)
density	*noun*	thickness; the amount of something in a given space (page 34)
deported	*verb*	carried or sent away; forced someone to leave a country (page 38)
descendants	*noun*	people of a later generation of a family or group (page 28)
destination	*noun*	the place where someone is going (page 98)
devise	*verb*	to invent; to think up (page 94)
dignifies	*verb*	makes noble or worthy (page 54)
dignity	*noun*	the state of being respected or honored (page 55)
dilute	*verb*	to thin down a mixture by the addition of water or another liquid; to lessen the strength or effect of something (page 15)
dilutions	*noun*	mixtures thinned down by the addition of water or another liquid (page 8)
disadvantage	*noun*	an unfavorable circumstance (page 84)
disadvantaged	*adjective*	lacking basic resources, such as food and housing (page 78)
dispose (of)	*verb*	to get rid (of) (page 16)
distinctly	*adjective*	without question, definitely (page 94)
divert	*verb*	to turn aside (page 45)
donations	*noun*	gifts or contributions (page 78)

E

earphones	*noun*	listening devices worn over the ears (page 94)
effective	*adjective*	having an effect; producing the desired result; making a striking impression (page 9)
effectively	*adverb*	in a way that produces the desired result (page 15)
electrical	*adjective*	having to do with electricity (page 94)
electron	*adjective*	made up of the very small particles that carry electricity (page 94)
elevations	*noun*	heights (page 98)
eligible	*adjective*	qualified; fit to be chosen (page 54)
endear	*verb*	to make dear or beloved (page 38)
ethnic	*adjective*	having to do with religious, racial, national, or cultural groups (page 84)
evoke	*verb*	to call forth; to bring out (page 84)
excavation	*noun*	digging (page 34)
exceeded	*verb*	went beyond (page 24)
excursion	*noun*	a usually short trip; a group of people on a short trip together; a temporary change of direction or topic (pages 98, 102)
exposure	*noun*	contact; being seen or known (page 84)
expressive	*adjective*	showing many emotions (page 84)

F

factor	*noun*	an element or ingredient (page 9)
fascinating	*adjective*	inspiring a lot of interest (page 98)
floundered	*verb*	struggled awkwardly; acted with confusion and hesitation (page 38)
forebears	*noun*	ancestors; people in the line of parents that led to the present generation (page 28)
formidable	*adjective*	fearsome; difficult to overcome (page 104)

H

habitat	*noun*	region where a plant or animal naturally lives (page 8)
harness	*verb*	to control in order to make use of (page 18)
heroic	*adjective*	having great courage (page 55)
heroism	*noun*	bravery, especially in a dangerous situation (page 54)
historic	*adjective*	very important; likely to be remembered for a long time (page 75)
humankind	*noun*	all the people living on Earth (page 24)

I

illusion	*noun*	something that seems to be real but is not (page 94)
immersed	*adjective*	completely covered by a liquid (page 34)
immortality	*noun*	the state of living forever (page 54)
immune	*adjective*	free from something unpleasant; resistant to disease (page 15)
immunity	*noun*	freedom from something unpleasant; resistance to a particular disease; exemption (pages 9, 88)
impassable	*adjective*	impossible to travel through (page 104)
impervious	*adjective*	incapable of being passed through or penetrated (page 34)
impose	*verb*	to force (page 16)
impossibility	*noun*	something that cannot happen or be (page 24)
impostor	*noun*	someone pretending to be somebody else to cheat or fool (page 16)
inappropriate	*adjective*	not suitable or proper (page 65)
incomprehensible	*adjective*	not able to be understood (page 48)
indelibly	*adverb*	permanently; in a way that cannot be erased or removed (page 74)
indescribable	*adjective*	not able to be described or put into words (page 68)
inefficiently	*adverb*	in a way that does not make the best use of something (page 65)
infectious	*adjective*	capable of causing an infection; spreading or able to spread from one person to another; capable of being easily spread (pages 88, 91)
inhabit	*verb*	to live in (pages 15, 65)
inhabitant	*noun*	person or animal that lives in a certain place or area (page 15)
inject	*verb*	to force a liquid into the body (page 65)
inoperative	*adjective*	not functioning properly (page 65)
inscribed	*verb*	carved letters or symbols in a hard surface (page 74)
instill	*verb*	to teach little by little (page 84)

instinctively	*adverb*	without thinking; by instinct (page 104)
intangible	*adjective*	vague; not easily defined (page 59)
invert	*verb*	to turn upside down (page 45)
involvement	*noun*	the act of taking part (page 84)

J

jostled	*verb*	bumped or pushed, as in a crowd (page 59)
jubilant	*adjective*	joyful; elated (page 38)
jubilee	*noun*	a time of celebration (page 44)

K

kinetic	*adjective*	having to do with motion (page 18)

L

laborious	*adjective*	requiring long, hard work (page 34)
latitudes	*noun*	imaginary circles drawn around Earth at a given distance from the North or South Pole (page 28)
lethal	*adjective*	deadly (page 9)
lightweight	*adjective*	weighing very little (page 18)

M

mapping	*noun*	the act of making a drawing, or map, of a place (page 68)
mechanized	*adjective*	machine-run (page 18)
mementos	*noun*	reminders or souvenirs (page 38)
merged	*verb*	blended together (page 104)
microorganisms	*noun*	tiny organisms, such as viruses or bacteria, that can be seen only under a microscope (page 88)
migrants	*noun*	people who move from one place to another, often in order to settle there; wanderers (page 28)
migration	*noun*	movement from one place to settle in another place (page 30)
milestone	*noun*	an important event (page 54)
miniature	*adjective*	very small (page 94)
modified	*verb*	changed (page 18)
monarchy	*noun*	a country ruled by one ruler, such as a king, queen, or emperor (page 21)
monochromatic	*adjective*	having, or perceived as having, only one color (page 21)
monocle	*noun*	an eyeglass for correcting the vision around one eye (page 21)
monogrammed	*adjective*	designed with one or more letters, usually initials of a name (page 21)
monoplane	*noun*	an aircraft that has only one set of wings (page 18)
monotone	*noun*	a sound that does not rise and fall in pitch but instead stays on the same tone (page 21)
monotonous	*adjective*	boring because of being repetitive and unvaried (page 98)

monumental	*adjective*	huge or enormous in size; very important (pages 48, 50)
motivation	*noun*	thing that makes a person act; desire or drive (page 68)
multiple	*adjective*	numerous; having many parts (page 8)

N

nomad	*noun*	member of a group that does not have a fixed home; wanderer (page 30)
nomadic	*adjective*	wandering; having no fixed home (page 28)
nontoxic	*adjective*	not poisonous; harmless (page 15)
nucleus	*noun*	the center of something, around which other things are grouped or collected (page 38)

O

operation	*noun*	the state of being functional or in effect; a medical procedure that involves surgery; an organized action, especially one carried out by the police or military; a mathematical process, for example, subtraction, addition, or multiplication; an illegal or dishonest business (pages 98, 101)
operative	*adjective*	in effect; capable of being used (page 38)
opponent	*noun*	someone who is against a particular action or belief; a rival (page 16)
overseas	*adjective*	across an ocean (page 24)

P

particular	*adjective*	distinct; specific (page 8)
passageway	*noun*	a way to get from one place to another (page 68)
pathogens	*noun*	things that can cause disease, such as a virus (page 88)
perilous	*adjective*	dangerous (page 88)
perseverance	*noun*	steady action or belief, usually over a long period of time (page 78)
perspective	*noun*	point of view (page 74)
platform	*noun*	a raised structure at a rail station where passengers can board and others can wait for passengers; a raised level of flooring for performers or speakers; the policies of a political party seeking election; a computer operating system; a position of authority or fame that provides a good opportunity for doing something (pages 98, 101)
poised	*verb*	balanced; kept steady (page 58)
portable	*adjective*	easily carried (page 94)
portray	*verb*	to describe using words, pictures, or actions (page 75)
portrayals	*noun*	descriptions of something in the form of language or a picture (page 74)
precautions	*noun*	things done beforehand to prevent trouble (page 68)
precipice	*noun*	a very steep cliff (page 104)

preconceptions	*noun*	ideas of something formed before one has all the facts (page 74)
prehistoric	*adjective*	happening before the time of recorded history; earlier than about 5,000 B.C. (page 74)
preliminary	*adjective*	preparatory; leading up to the main action (page 9)
pretense	*noun*	something that lacks genuineness (page 44)
pretentious	*adjective*	pompous; acting more important or special than other people (page 44)
probable	*adjective*	likely; believable (page 28)
productive	*adjective*	having positive results; effective (page 34)
profile	*noun*	the outline of someone's face, seen from the side; a short account of someone's life or activities; a level of how noticeable someone or something is (pages 98, 102)
profile	*verb*	to write or present a short account of someone's life or activities (page 102)
profit	*noun*	income from an investment or a business (page 44)
profitable	*adjective*	moneymaking; beneficial (page 38)
prompted	*verb*	urged (page 8)
promptness	*noun*	being on time; being at the appointed time (page 15)
proponent	*noun*	someone who argues for or wants something (page 16)
proportion	*noun*	a part or share of the whole (page 8)
proportional	*adjective*	in the correct relationship of size, quantity, or degree to something else (page 15)
proposal	*noun*	a suggestion, often made formally; a marriage offer (page 15)
proposes	*verb*	puts forth for consideration; plans; presents as a toast; nominates for office or membership; offers marriage (page 9)
prospector	*noun*	a person who searches for gold or other valuable things buried in the earth (page 68)
prospered	*verb*	succeeded; flourished (page 38)
prosperous	*adjective*	wealthy and successful (page 78)

Q

quietude	*noun*	calmness (page 59)
quips	*noun*	witty or sarcastic remarks (page 38)

R

radiation	*noun*	energy emitted from a source in the form of rays or waves (page 88)
random	*adjective*	haphazard (page 38)
recognition	*noun*	credit or appreciation (page 78)
remote	*adjective*	isolated; distant (page 58)
remoteness	*noun*	the quality of being distant or secluded (page 64)
repose	*noun*	rest; sleep; composure; calm (page 59)

resilience	*noun*	the ability to spring back into shape or to recover strength or good spirits quickly (page 64)
resilient	*adjective*	bouncing or springing back into original shape or form (page 58)
resistance	*noun*	the act of withstanding or opposing; opposition to something or somebody (pages 8, 78)
reverse	*verb*	to turn backward (page 45)
revert	*verb*	to return to a former practice, opinion, or state (page 38)
rigid	*adjective*	not bending or flexible (page 58)
rigidity	*noun*	the quality of being inflexible (page 64)
rodent	*noun*	group of mammals that includes mice, rats, and squirrels (page 8)

S

scrutinize	*verb*	to examine closely; to look at in detail (page 75)
scrutiny	*noun*	close examination (page 74)
situated	*verb*	located (page 48)
somnolent	*adjective*	sleepy, drowsy; causing drowsiness (page 59)
spelunking	*noun*	the exploration of caves (page 68)
spirit	*noun*	a frame of mind or disposition; life principle or soul; liveliness; courage; an apparition (page 59)
spiritual	*adjective*	having to do with the soul or spirit (page 65)
strait	*noun*	a narrow waterway that connects two larger bodies of water (page 28)
surgical	*adjective*	having to do with medical operations (page 88)
surmount	*verb*	to climb to the top of; to overcome (page 104)
symbolic	*adjective*	standing for something else (page 48)
sympathize	*verb*	to share the feelings or ideas of another; to express pity or compassion for another (page 38)
sympathy	*noun*	the ability to feel compassion for someone else (page 44)

T

tangible	*adjective*	having actual form or substance; able to be touched (page 64)
tariffs	*noun*	taxes placed by a government on exports or imports (page 38)
temperament	*noun*	disposition (page 8)
toxic	*adjective*	poisonous (page 15)
toxin	*noun*	poison (page 9)
transformed	*verb*	changed (page 98)
transmit	*verb*	to send out (page 24)
travail	*noun*	very hard work; intense pain (page 59)
turbulence	*noun*	violence of motion; uproar (page 64)
turbulent	*adjective*	wild; stormy; disorderly (page 58)

U

uninhabited	*adjective*	without people; empty (page 28)
unpretentious	*adjective*	modest and simple (page 38)

V

vaccine	*noun*	a substance that helps your body develop immunity to a disease (page 88)
venom	*noun*	the poison secreted by some snakes, spiders, insects, etc. (page 8)
verge	*noun*	the edge or brink of something (page 58)
vertical	*adjective*	upright; perpendicular to the horizon (page 58)
veterans	*noun*	those who have served in the armed forces (page 54)
visual	*adjective*	having to do with things that are seen (page 94)
visualize	*verb*	to picture in one's mind (page 74)

W

warranted	*verb*	justified or deserved (page 38)
warranty	*noun*	guarantee (page 44)

Z

zenith	*noun*	the point in the sky directly overhead; the highest point (page 104)

Vocabulary in Context G9, SV 9780547625829

Answer Key

Pages 10–11

1. B	11. B
2. C	12. B
3. C	13. B
4. B	14. D
5. C	15. A
6. A	16. B
7. D	17. A
8. C	18. B
9. A	19. C
10. A	20. C

Page 12

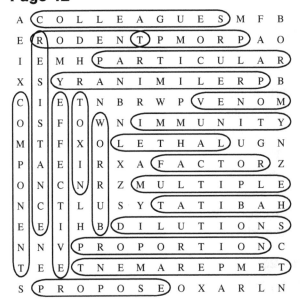

Page 13

1. C	6. A
2. C	7. B
3. A	8. A
4. A	9. C
5. D	10. A

Page 14

1. c
2. a
3. b
4. b
5. c
6. a
7. d

8. a
9. b
10. c

Page 15

1. dilute
2. inhabitant
3. promptness
4. immune
5. toxic
6. inhabit
7. proposal
8. effectively
9. proportional
10. nontoxic

Page 16
The Latin Root *pon/pos*

1. B
2. D
3. A
4. E
5. C

Completing Sentences

1. impose
2. impostor
3. opponent
4. dispose
5. proponent

Page 17

Answers will vary based on students' personal experiences.

Page 19

1. mechanized
2. modified
3. kinetic
4. accelerated
5. monoplane
6. lightweight
7. conducted
8. altimeter

8. harness

10. accessible

Page 20
Understanding Multiple-Meanings Words

1. f
2. b
3. c
4. h
5. d
6. a
7. g
8. e

Cloze Paragraphs

1. accessible
2. monoplane
3. accelerated
4. altimeter
5. kinetic

Page 21
Synonyms and Antonyms

1. Synonyms
2. Antonyms
3. Antonyms
4. Synonyms
5. Antonyms

The Greek Root *mono*

1. monocle
2. monarchy
3. monotone
4. monochromatic
5. monogrammed

Page 22
Word Game

1. harness
2. accelerated
3. modified
4. lightweight
5. accessible

Challenge Yourself

Answers may vary. Sample answers are provided.

1. the wind, the sun
2. the settings on my word processing program, my essay
3. a washing machine

Page 23

1. A
2. B
3. C
4. C
5. B
6. D
7. A
8. D
9. D
10. C

Page 24

1. humankind
2. transmit
3. contraptions
4. Amazingly
5. impossibility
6. clarity
7. closeness
8. overseas
9. correspondence
10. exceeded

Page 25
Antonyms

1. closeness
2. overseas
3. impossibility
4. amazingly
5. clarity
6. transmit

Writing Sentences

Answers will vary. Sample answers are provided.

1. We explained to Grandma that the contraptions around our necks were MP3 players.
2. In my correspondence to the committee, I explained why I wanted the city to consider making one of the parks leash-free for dogs.

3. I thought the movie would be dull, but it far exceeded my expectations; it was action-packed and fun.
4. His hope is that all of humankind will know happiness and peace.

Page 26

1. C
2. A
3. A
4. D
5. B
6. C
7. D
8. D
9. A
10. C

Page 27

Answers will vary based on students' personal experiences.

Page 29

1. probable
2. adjacent
3. nomadic
4. latitudes
5. migrants
6. uninhabited
7. forebears
8. descendants
9. demonstrated
10. strait

Page 30

Analogies

1. adjacent
2. strait
3. forebears
4. probable
5. uninhabited

Word Pairs

Answers may vary. Sample answers are provided.

1. The migrant moved from Sweden to Norway.

There is a migration of bats into Austin, Texas, every year.
2. I will demonstrate how to use the new game.
While Uncle George tends to be demonstrative at family gatherings, Aunt Shari keeps her feelings to herself.
3. The nomad joined her group in getting ready for the next move.
She does not have a nomadic lifestyle; she's lived in the same house for 12 years.

Page 31

1. adjacent
2. strait
3. latitudes
4. forebears
5. nomadic
6. demonstrated
7. probable
8. descendants
9. uninhabited
10. migrants

Page 32

Across

3. probable
6. descendants
7. strait
8. latitudes
10. nomadic

Down

1. forebears
2. demonstrated
4. adjacent
5. migrants
9. uninhabited

Page 33

1. B
2. C
3. D
4. A
5. D
6. C
7. B
8. A

Vocabulary in Context G9, SV 9780547625829

9. B
10. A

Page 34

1. excavation
2. casualties
3. bedrock
4. comprises
5. density
6. airtight
7. impervious
8. immersed
9. laborious
10. productive

Page 35
Synonyms and Antonyms

1. Antonyms
2. Synonyms
3. Antonyms
4. Synonyms
5. Antonyms

Dictionary Skills

1. comprises, a
2. excavation, a
3. density, b
4. laborious, b
5. bedrock, b

Page 36

1. A
2. C
3. B
4. D
5. C
6. D
7. A
8. D
9. C
10. B

Page 37

Answers will vary based on students' personal experiences.

Pages 40–41

1. D
2. A
3. A
4. B
5. A
6. B
7. C
8. D
9. A
10. D
11. B
12. C
13. A
14. C
15. A
16. C
17. B
18. B
19. C
20. D

Page 42
Matching Ideas

1. floundered
2. random
3. deported
4. prosper
5. memento

True-False

1. F
2. F
3. T
4. F
5. T
6. T
7. T
8. F
9. F
10. T

Page 43

1. C
2. B
3. A
4. A
5. C
6. D
7. B
8. B
9. C
10. A
11. B
12. B

Page 44

Understanding Related Words
1. profit, profitable
2. jubilant, jubilee
3. pretentious, pretense
4. sympathized, sympathy
5. warrants, warranty

Dictionary Skills
1. sym-pa-thy
2. ju-bi-lee
3. war-ran-ty
4. pre-ten-tious
5. bel-lig-er-ent
6. con-temp-tu-ous

Page 45

The Latin Root *vert*
1. invert
2. convert
3. reverse
4. controversy
5. divert

Challenge Yourself
Answers may vary. Sample answers are provided.
1. sell something I own, make and sell lemonade
2. when my friend hurt her shoulder, when my mom lost her bracelet
3. a radio, a computer

Page 46

Word Pairs
1. profit
2. controversy
3. sympathy
4. warranty
5. pretense

Forming Words
Answers may vary. Sample answers are provided.

rent, trip, risen, print, tent, sent, teen, seen, prose, rose

Page 47

Answers will vary based on students' personal experiences.

Page 49
1. citadel
2. situated
3. artistry
4. colonize
5. cumbersome
6. monumental
7. symbolic
8. incomprehensible
9. commemorate
10. adornments

Page 50

Understanding Multiple-Meaning Words
1. a
2. b
3. b
4. a

Word Groups
1. colonize
2. artistry
3. incomprehensible
4. cumbersome
5. symbolic
6. commemorate
7. adornments
8. citadel
9. monumental
10. situate

Page 51

Answers may vary. Sample answers are provided. Vocabulary words are italicized.

What We See
1. *adornments*
2. *artistry*
3. *monumental*
4. *cumbersome*
5. jutting chins

Purpose of the Statues

1. *symbolic*
2. *citadel*
3. *commemorate*
4. protection
5. decoration

Reactions to the Statues

1. *incomprehensible*
2. impressive
3. awe-inspiring
4. exciting
5. confusing

Page 52
Synonyms and Antonyms

1. Antonyms
2. Synonyms
3. Antonyms
4. Antonyms
5. Synonyms

The Suffixes *-able* and *-ible*

1. notable
2. laughable
3. sensible
4. permissible
5. reusable
6. excusable
7. comfortable
8. permissible
9. adjustable
10. deductible

Page 53

1. C
2. D
3. D
4. B
5. B
6. C
7. B
8. A
9. C
10. C

Page 54

1. dignifies
2. completion
3. veterans
4. heroism
5. immortality
6. architecture
7. authorized
8. milestone
9. eligible
10. creativity

Page 55
Word Groups

1. heroism
2. authorized
3. veterans
4. dignifies
5. eligible
6. creativity
7. architecture
8. milestone

Word Pairs

Answers will vary. Sample answers are provided.

1. My new painting is my greatest creation yet.
   In our writing group, we learn how to access our creativity.
2. It was heroic of the little girl to call 911 when she saw fire in the kitchen.
   Our armed services are full of men and women committed to heroism.
3. We should treat all people with dignity, no matter what we think of them.
   A war memorial dignifies the soldiers who fought in the battle.
4. The teacher authorized an extra ten minutes for lunch.
   I do not have authorization to allow you into the building.

Page 56

1. B
2. D
3. A

Vocabulary in Context G9, SV 9780547625829

4. C
5. D
6. B
7. A
8. C
9. D
10. A

Page 57

Answers will vary based on students' personal experiences.

Pages 60–61

1. C	**11.** B
2. D	**12.** C
3. D	**13.** A
4. C	**14.** C
5. A	**15.** A
6. A	**16.** C
7. D	**17.** C
8. D	**18.** B
9. B	**19.** A
10. B	**20.** A

Page 62
Using Context Clues

1. A
2. B
3. C
4. B
5. B

Figures of Speech

1. personification
2. simile
3. metaphor
4. personification

Page 63

1. D	**8.** B
2. A	**9.** B
3. B	**10.** A
4. C	**11.** D
5. B	**12.** C
6. C	**13.** B
7. C	**14.** B

Page 64

1. ceaseless
2. resilience
3. arresting
4. turbulence
5. tangible
6. abrupt
7. remoteness
8. chaotic
9. rigidity
10. austere

Page 65
Answering Questions About Words

1. D
2. B
3. B
4. A
5. C

The Prefix *in-*

1. inhabit
2. inoperative
3. inappropriate
4. inject
5. inefficiently

Page 66

1. b
2. a
3. c
4. a
5. b
6. b
7. a
8. b
9. b

Page 67

Answers will vary based on students' personal experiences.

Page 69

1. spelunking
2. adventurers
3. motivation
4. precautions

Vocabulary in Context G9, SV 9780547625829

5. attire
6. dank
7. passageway
8. mapping
9. indescribable
10. prospector

Page 70
Dictionary Skills
1. mapping, b
2. attire, a
3. prospector, a
4. precaution, b

Rewriting Sentences
1. His need for money was his motivation to work.
2. The air is dank in the cellar.
3. As a hobby, you can't beat spelunking for excitement.
4. My brother is the only true adventurer in our family.
5. The dinner was so delicious that it was indescribable.

Page 71
Answers may vary. Sample answers are provided. Vocabulary words are italicized.

Who Might Explore a Cave
1. *adventurers*
2. *prospectors*
3. spelunkers
4. cave lovers
5. scientists

What Spelunkers See
1. *passageways*
2. stalactites
3. jagged rocks
4. falling dirt
5. unusual rocks

What Spelunkers Need
1. *motivation*
2. *attire*
3. ropes
4. courage

5. common sense

Why Spelunkers Explore
1. fun
2. adventure
3. discoveries
4. excitement
5. studying

Page 72
Yes or No?
1. no
2. yes
3. yes
4. no
5. no
6. no
7. no

Challenge Yourself
Answers may vary. Sample answers are provided.
1. putting on a raincoat, finding an umbrella
2. parasailing, rock climbing
3. when giving directions, when hiking on a new path

Page 73
1. D
2. C
3. D
4. A
5. B
6. C
7. B
8. C
9. A
10. D

Page 74
1. preconceptions
2. prehistoric
3. perspective
4. authenticate
5. scrutiny
6. visualize
7. portrayals

8. inscribed
9. attribute
10. indelibly

Page 75
Analogies
1. prehistoric
2. indelibly
3. perspective
4. authenticate
5. inscribed
6. visualize
7. scrutiny

Word Pairs

Answers will vary. Sample answers are provided.

1. The famous painting came under close scrutiny after rumors spread that it was a fake.
Reporters scrutinize the released reports, looking for evidence of wrongdoing.
2. My favorite actor will portray the president in the upcoming miniseries.
Her portrayal of the queen in her latest book was fascinating.
3. She conceptualized her novel years before she actually began writing.
Some people have a preconception that all science is dull and are pleasantly surprised to learn it can be fascinating.
4. The archaeologists found items thought to be prehistoric in their last dig.
The presidential inauguration was a historic event; people will be discussing it for years to come.

Page 76
1. scrutiny
2. prehistoric
3. preconceptions
4. portrayal
5. inscribed
6. indelibly
7. visualize
8. attribute
9. perspective

10. authenticate

Page 77
Answers will vary based on students' personal experiences.

Page 79
1. prosperous
2. recognition
3. benefactor
4. commendable
5. benefits
6. donations
7. perseverance
8. disadvantaged
9. benevolence
10. resistance

Page 80
1. benefits
2. disadvantaged
3. benevolence
4. perseverance
5. donations
6. recognition
7. benefactor
8. resistance
9. commendable
10. prosperous

Page 81
1. b
2. a
3. d
4. c
5. b
6. a
7. b
8. a

Page 82
True-False
1. F
2. F
3. T
4. F
5. T

6. T
7. F
8. T

Challenge Yourself

Answers may vary. Sample answers are provided.

1. sharing a snack, giving up your seat on the bus
2. finished my homework, washed and dried the dishes
3. expensive car, nice house

Page 83

1. B
2. A
3. C
4. B
5. B
6. D
7. D
8. C
9. D
10. B

Page 84

1. confined
2. exposure
3. ethnic
4. instill
5. disadvantage
6. conventional
7. expressive
8. evoke
9. involvement
10. acceptance

Page 85
Antonyms

1. expressive
2. disadvantage
3. confined
4. acceptance
5. conventional
6. evoke
7. instill

Name Game

Answers may vary. Sample answers are provided.

1. getting to work on time, doing a good job
2. driving a car, riding the bus
3. joining a softball team, going to city council meetings
4. hitting a home run, catching a fly ball

Page 86
Word Origins

1. acceptance
2. exposure
3. evoke
4. confined
5. instill
6. ethnic

Writing Sentences

Answers may vary. Sample answers are provided.

1. She received her college acceptance letter last week.
2. The new ruling worked to our disadvantage.
3. Saying "hello" is the conventional way to answer the telephone.
4. Instead of being expressive, he just sat quietly.
5. The reporter's exposure of their crimes led to an arrest.
6. I had no involvement in the play because I had to work every night.

Page 87

Answers will vary based on students' personal experiences.

Page 89

1. vaccine
2. radiation
3. contrived
4. antibiotic
5. immunity
6. perilous
7. microorganisms
8. infectious

9. surgical
10. pathogens

Page 90
Rewriting Sentences

1. Ultraviolet radiation is used to prevent illnesses at hospitals.
2. He contrived a clever method for cleaning hospital rooms.
3. To prevent the spread of smallpox, doctors gave their patients a vaccine.
4. After getting a sinus infection, William got a prescription for an antibiotic.
5. The laboratory contained samples of many different types of pathogens.

True-False

1. F
2. T
3. F
4. F
5. T

Page 91

1. a
2. c
3. b
4. b
5. a
6. a
7. b

Page 92
Word Groups

1. immunity
2. microorganisms
3. contrived
4. infectious
5. perilous

Challenge Yourself

Answers may vary. Sample answers are provided.

1. traveling overseas, before starting a new school
2. nurse, orderly
3. microscope

Page 93

1. A
2. C
3. B
4. D
5. A
6. C
7. B
8. D
9. C
10. D

Page 94

1. distinctly
2. portable
3. electrical
4. contrast
5. visual
6. electron
7. devise
8. earphones
9. miniature
10. illusion

Page 95
Antonyms

1. distinctly
2. portable
3. miniature

Dictionary Skills

1. devise, a
2. electron, b
3. contrast, a
4. illusion, a
5. distinctly, b
6. electrical, b

Page 96

1. B
2. C
3. D
4. B
5. C
6. A
7. C
8. D

9. A
10. B

Page 97

Answers will vary based on students' personal experiences.

Page 99

1. cascading
2. fascinating
3. destination
4. transformed
5. elevations
6. operation
7. profiles
8. monotonous
9. platform
10. excursion

Page 100

1. fascinating
2. elevations
3. transformed
4. destination
5. operation
6. monotonous
7. profiles
8. excursions
9. platform
10. cascading

Pages 101–102

1. e	11. c
2. b	12. a
3. a	13. d
4. c	14. b
5. d	15. b
6. e	16. a
7. d	17. c
8. c	18. b
9. a	19. a
10. b	20. c

Page 103

1. B
2. C
3. B
4. D
5. B
6. D
7. A
8. C
9. D
10. B

Page 104

1. formidable
2. committed
3. surmount
4. precipice
5. abyss
6. impassable
7. merged
8. instinctively
9. bracing
10. zenith

Page 105

Analogies

1. committed
2. formidable
3. abyss
4. precipice
5. surmount
6. merged

Word Descriptions

1. bracing
2. impassable
3. surmount
4. zenith
5. instinctively

Page 106

1. D	6. D
2. A	7. C
3. C	8. D
4. A	9. C
5. A	10. A

Page 107

Answers will vary based on students' personal experiences.

Printed in the USA
CPSIA information can be obtained
at www.ICGtesting.com
LVHW080248110224
771466LV00009B/101